Up and About

The Memoir of an Expatriate Spouse

KEMI OLOIDI

ISBN: 978-978-790-866-2

I have tried to recreate events, locales and conversations from my memories of them. In order to maintain their anonymity in some instances I have changed the names of individuals and places, I may have changed some identifying characteristics and details such as physical properties, occupations and places of residence.

Edited and Published by SW Advantage Resources; www.sw-advantage.com, edits@sw-advantage.com, +2348037741008.

'Our homes are not defined by geography or one particular location, but by memories, events, people and places that span the globe'.

~ Marilyn Gardner

This book is dedicated to

My late parents for being instrumental to who I am today; their love and discipline shaped my life.

My wonderful husband for carrying me along every step of the way. You are the best man in the whole wide world!

My wonderful children for being the best—no tantrums, no drama. We all looked out for each other.

And finally, Procter and Gamble for the opportunity given to my family to see the world.

Acknowledgements

My first appreciation is to God Almighty, the giver of life through whom all inspirations come. To Him alone do all glory belong.

Writing a book is harder than I thought and more rewarding than I could have ever imagined. None of this would have been possible without the numerous people who encouraged me to put my experiences down in writing. Indeed, it is with their push and encouragement that I have written this book. To you all, I say thank you.

Naty Tully, my friend and pastor's wife in Bucharest; you stood by me during the very early stages of this book, gave useful advice, and helped me to bring life into the boring pieces of the first drafts. Thank you, Naty. Though we could not finish the book together, I understand the situation and your valued commitments in other areas to both your community and the church of God. I'm praying for you, your family, and the world.

I'm eternally grateful to my niece, Mrs. Kumbi Ajonibadi (née Dixon); you also worked on the initial manuscripts that would now make the book very interesting to read. Thank you, Kumbi for your tremendous help. I appreciate when I had to call you late at night and make you run with my own schedule even while nursing your little baby.

A very special thanks to a good man, Mr. Seun Oluwole, our dear friend and brother. We lived together in Belgium. Thank you for helping me polish every bit of this work. Your ideas and suggestions added meaning to this book and your work ethic is very impressive. Thank you, sir; I appreciate your love for my family and me.

I sincerely appreciate Mr. Wale Adediran, my own very special brother. Thank you for everything. You were there in the beginning and are still standing by us despite many years of living apart. You agreed without any hesitation to write the foreword to the book in spite of your very busy schedule. Thank you very much for creating time to read my book before it was published. I feel honoured, sir.

Special thanks to all the women who stood by me and with whom I did life together even when it was hard: my walk buddies, my book club ladies, the ICWA women in Brussels and my many church friends and ministry leads in all the different countries. Thank you all for the love, care, and opportunities.

Writing a book about a portion of one's life is a surreal process. I'm forever indebted to the SW Advantage team for their editorial help, keen insight, and ongoing support in bringing my stories to life. I am especially grateful to Ini Akpan and Ofoegbu Chinedu for their commitment to get everything right.

To my husband, my very own S.O., my number one supporter and go-to person; you were always reminding me of things that I either forgot or chose not to write about. Thank you for giving me a free hand to put our stories out in the open. I trust I haven't given away too many of the escapades. Thank you for making me believe I am a queen even when I didn't feel like one. Your steadfast love and trust give me the wings to fly. You sustain me in ways that I never knew I needed. I love you with all my heart, and I thank you specially.

To my Dammy and LiliB, thank you for trusting our parenting skills and making those years easy on your dad and me. Thank you for encouraging and pushing me to write my story no matter how I feel about it; you two made me feel like I was a superstar. Thank you for your wise words, the cheering up and for those periods that we did many things together. I remember our France hangout, getting lost and finding the way together; I thank you both for being the anchor. Thanks for adding to the book. Thank you for letting me know that you had nothing but great memories of me as a young mother. So thankful to have you both in my life.

Finally, to all those who have been a part of my getting here. My uncle Alhaji Amusa, Dr. Dixon and his wife Auntie Telle, Engr. Afolabi Dixon and his wives — Alhaja Ganiat and Auntie Lanre; you served as our backbone during those years. Wasiu Amusa my very dear brother, your calls and occasional tete-a-tete are indeed life-giving.

The following deserve special mention: Akinola

Dixon, Sandra Black — thank you for reminding me of all I had forgotten, Ida Edwards — thank you for the pictures, Jonathan CrispMoore — thank you for permission to use our pictures, Pastor William Tully, Pastor Scott Parmenter, Tobi Bello — thank you for the recommendation, Ebube Nzom — thank you for your contribution, and Ifedayo Adeleye — thank you for your feedback. Thank you, all; I appreciate all your contributions and I wish you all well in your various endeavours.

What Some Readers Said

I recommend this book to all and sundry, particularly to those who love traveling in spite of the challenge of encountering different cultures, traditions and languages spoken in different parts of the world.

This book by Mrs. Kemi Oloidi is a tour guide in its entirety, giving assurance and hope to people who love to travel and even to those who don't like traveling but do so by obligation. Some people even have phobia for traveling or leaving their comfort zones but reading through this book will give you vivid pictures and ideas on how to tackle the challenges that may surface when the time comes, as also experienced by the author.

This book has really shown me that God has different plans for different people; black or white, race is inconsequential. All we need do is release our hands for the Lord to grab and lead us through life's journey.

I got so immersed in reading through that I found myself in the different countries, feeling the hostility in some, while relishing the amazing love shown by others, through the descriptions of the author.

I must finally salute her husband who thought it beautiful to carry his wife along in all the trips he had to take, not leaving her and their children at home while he globetrotted alone. Christ truly has made a difference in the lives of members of this family.

'And the two shall become one' has really been exhibited in this family, and it is a lesson for all to emulate.

Mrs. Adewunmi Lynda Aluko
Broadcaster with Federal Radio Corporation of Nigeria

This book narrates the experiences of an expatriate's wife. It is a wife's account from personal knowledge on managing a family and raising children while accompanying a spouse on overseas work assignments for extended periods.

The author succinctly explained her relocation using a linear style in capturing the visual imagery of her experiences and the dynamics of events that happened in her years of working and living in eight countries as well as her visits to different parts of the world.

The author stated the importance of marriage as an essential institution in the society, work-life balance, and the challenges of bringing up children while navigating life in a foreign country.

She explained the gulf between the realities and fantasies of living abroad through her own experiences.

The author advised prospective trailing spouses to learn how to properly situate themselves in any culture they might eventually find themselves. To the author, the key message is for the accompanying spouses to do some analysis and consider the pros and cons of living overseas before setting out.

The author narrated that faith keeps hope alive and

her faith as a believer in Christ was and still is an anchor for her and her family. She wrote about the turbulence and trials of loneliness and its attendant effects on the human mind. She enjoined that physical activities, social engagements and beliefs are crucial to life.

Kemi also wrote about racism, emphasizing that racism is real and that there are a lot of biases out there in the world. She specially narrowed it down to the double standards of the media, the failures of our governments and the ignorance of many people. She explained how she was able to confront this in her own subtle and sometimes dramatic ways. Nobody moving abroad should be naive about this.

She wrote extensively about life, the pleasures and emoluments of working and living as expatriates, her extensive travels, her rich understanding of the world culture and the gains of travel. Because of her exposure she could communicate moderately in other languages and appreciate the benefits of social engagements.

However, home is home. The author and her husband returned to Nigeria after meritorious overseas work assignments that spanned over 23 years.

Her tips and advice at the end of every chapter on how to manage and deal with relocation, living and working abroad is super. Similarly, the first-person narrative technique and the depth of her storytelling skills are the major factors that would make this book a compelling reading.

'Seun Oluwole, FCIPM
CEO, Tifor Business Solutions Limited
Former HR Manager, Mobil Producing Nigeria Unlimited

Contents

Foreword

It is such a great honour to present the foreword to this highly outstanding intellectual contribution to the global talent mobility resource pool. As a human resource management professional and an ardent follower of the shared professional and life careers of the author and her spouse, I must state upfront that I was looking forward to this crucial contribution. I am also pleasantly surprised to be so accorded the honour of making this testimonial contribution.

The author is my highly respected sister, and her amiable husband is my dear friend, professional colleague and now, becoming a trusted partner on life-changing ideas. His career has been an inspiration for many of us, his colleagues and former colleagues at the Procter and Gamble Corporation. The bigger inspiration however is his darling wife's decision to dedicate her career to supporting her husband's career since he was first handed his first expatriate posting very early in his career with Procter and Gamble. That was about three decades ago, a time when it was rare to find helpful resources to prepare any spouse for such a career — yes, a challenging career it is! I can imagine how challenging it was for her to navigate that uncharted territory.

Strong in resolve and character, she had weathered the storm, ridden the tide, climbed the ladder of chaos and basked in occasional moments of resounding successes and divine victories to successfully lead her husband and their two lovely children (now enterprising young man and woman) to career and life successes. She journeyed through nations, far and remote, not only in geographical positions but also in cultural and faith inclinations. She kept her faith and I dare say, facilitated the lifting of her husband's faith to a higher level when they navigated those strange lands and territories with only themselves, their kids, and their faith to lean on. The results are highly outstanding — career accomplishment, spiritual self-discovery, and social impact! Her impact and that of her family on several families in their host countries and home country are innumerable and great testimonies that their voyage was God-ordained.

Beyond the spiritual angle to all these are practical steps and choices she made, which made possible the beautiful story she is about to tell. She was deliberate and often, her guardian angels led her into some of the decisions. There were moments of doubts and feeling at a loss — she will share the blueprints she followed in managing them all to get good results. I am highly privileged to be among the very first few beneficiaries of her memoir. There are so many nuggets that apply positively to even home country 'regional expatriation' (like some of us have been on). She had shared many of such in our various family engagements. As an unselfish well-wisher, I am glad she is now putting them and many more out here for all of us to benefit from. Her style of writing is plain and captivating, easy to follow and difficult to drop once you start reading her narration. She narrates her captivating stories in writing, the same way she does in face-to-face conversations. Free flowing and engaging, in the usual 'Honorary Grandma' style.

So, for those of you who are at that point of

decision: to be or not to be, worried about leaving your career to support your spouse's career as he or she moves on expatriation (international or regional), faced with the dilemma of shock episodes on an ongoing expatriation accompaniment, thinking of how you will raise your kids while your family moves across culture zones, faced with strange language challenges, or just confused about legal jurisdiction and others; here is the resource for you. Her story will inspire your decision to be right and lift your spirit to go for it.

Wale Adediran FCIPM, FNIMechE, MNSE, HRPL, NPOM
Group HR and General Services Director,
Flour MIlls of Nigeria Plc., Apapa, Lagos, Nigeria
Immediate Past President, Chartered Institute of Personnel Management of Nigeria (CIPM).

Introduction

'I can't think of anything that incites a greater sense of childlike wonder than to be in a country where you are ignorant of almost everything. Suddenly, you are five years old again. You cannot read anything, you have only the rudimentary sense of how things work, you can't even reliably cross a street without endangering your life. Your whole existence becomes a series of interesting guesses.'

The quote above by Bill Bryson accurately describes my journey as a trailing wife. One moment, I was leading a relatively normal life and the next, I was off traversing various countries with my family, learning anew how to navigate life in new cultures.

Before I had to pack up and travel the globe, I had an almost non-existent idea of what the life of an expatriate entailed. The journey proved to be an intense exposure and immersion into the realities of living in a world with diverse beliefs and cultures.

In writing this book, I decided to share my journey to help anyone who might find themselves where I was about two decades ago, with many questions begging for answers.

As the trailing spouse of an expatriate or someone planning to move to a foreign land, understand that the excitement of traveling abroad should not overshadow the reality of moving into new, uncharted territory. I believe my experiences and tips will help you make informed decisions about traveling and living abroad.

It doesn't end there. I hope that through this book, you will get to see the world through my eyes and understand the value of each individual you meet, regardless of race or gender. Dig in!

Chapter One

THE OPPORTUNITY

'Everything about the future is uncertain, but one thing is for sure, the Almighty has already planned all our tomorrows.'

~ Aashu

Well-travelled. Is that the best phrase that describes me? Probably.

You see, I was minding my business and enjoying a busy but peaceful life in Ibadan with my beloved husband when an opportunity that would take us across the world showed up.

One day, I was setting up my plans and enjoying the work I do as a civil servant, a wife and a mum with a side hustle. The next day, I was a foreigner grappling with new realities on foreign soil.

Everything changed before I could take a breather to savour my, no, our new fortune and destination.

It seemed like it was just the day before that we had arrived in Ibadan. Yes, I loved the idea of travelling to see the world but the way it happened came as a huge surprise.

At first, Lagos was home, then it was gone. Then Ibadan became home, and it was going too. I was lost. As a girl born and bred in Surulere, Lagos, to an Abeokuta mother and a full-fledged Lagosian father, Lagos was my home. That was where I went to school and grew up. Everything you could associate my life with was in Lagos. I had never stepped outside of Lagos, except for my three-year National Certificate in Education (NCE) programme in Oyo State.

I didn't like to move. I liked to stay with what I was used to so much that when my husband got a job in Ibadan and had to move (he moved a lot), I stayed back in Lagos while he shuttled back home every weekend. This happened for over six months.

Soon, it became uncomfortable for him because this was barely two years into our married life. He must have thought to himself, *No, I don't want to do this. I want to move my family to Ibadan to stay with me.*

Till today, I still don't know how he worked out my transfer because he brought the letter to me and said, 'This is your transfer letter; you're going to Ibadan.'

At that point, I had no excuse strong enough to keep me back because all along, I had used my job as a convenient reason to stay back. He gave me a two-day movement notice and we swiftly packed our bags and moved into our small apartment in Ring Road, Ibadan. That was in 1994.

We settled down in no time and life began to unfold, as nothing can stop life from rolling. We made new friends and I found a good hairdresser. Having a good hairdresser is and has always been important to me—it was a huge concern while moving.

Back in Lagos, I had worked with the Federal Ministry of Communication as an investigation officer, the same job that I was assigned when we arrived Ibadan. My job was to investigate postal fraud and theft. Just like there is internet fraud today, back then, there was postal fraud. People would send deliveries from abroad but sometimes, they would not get to the rightful owners. We worked with the Nigerian police to curtail that, and we made sure parcels got to their rightful owners. I did this job for nine years before the big move that began my overseas adventure.

Apart from my full-time job, I had a side business. The common notion is that working with the government is easy, but my job wasn't; it didn't give me much spare time. If I was not in the police station, I was either in court, busy preparing a case or writing a report.

In my side business, I sold Coca-Cola products. I had gotten the opportunity to rent a large store space and I had taken it. Over time, the business grew. Because of the demands of my job, I had to employ a salesperson. I got an honest boy who managed the store and from time to time, I would go to oversee the business. Also, my sister-in-law helped me oversee things in the store. When my first sales boy got admission for his part-time polytechnic studies, I had to hire another person to make them two. Whenever he wasn't available, the other would take over from him. With that arrangement, we were able to sustain the business.

To be honest, it's not easy being a working-class mother. I had challenges, especially during the summer months when the children were on holidays and I had to resume work by 0730 hours.

The children's playgroup often opened by 0900 hours, and I had to drop them off myself. Maintaining work-life balance was indeed a challenge. The situation almost caused a rift between my boss and me because I was often late to work.

However, I eventually managed to work my way around the challenges. I designed a special routine in which I would drop off my children at school or day care much earlier in the morning and pick them up later in the day on my way home.

With my children, my salaried job and my private business, I was having the time of my life. My husband was having a swell time, too. He couldn't have asked for a better job. Having made a habit of giving his best efforts to his job, he was getting a lot of recognition. My new home was built, and we were happy in it.

Life was going well, but after a while, it became obvious my husband wanted a new challenge. Even though his job was a very dynamic one, his daily routine was gradually becoming monotonous. He began to look forward to a new role, a new opportunity or something more challenging than the usual assignment. Aspiration became a longing and soon, we started looking for how to make that happen.

As expected, I stood by him to support his vision and dreams. We were both on the lookout. The daily newspapers became our daily companions, particularly the job advert sections. We found some interesting openings but the ones he applied to didn't yield anything tangible.

Then boom! The opportunity came when we least expected it. The best part was that not only was this the perfect opportunity he had been looking for, it also exceeded his expectations.

I vividly remember the night he told me about the new opportunity. He broke the news to me in the same romantic way that he had proposed marriage to me.

It was a Friday evening, and we were out for a night of food and drinks. Valentine was in the air, evident in the reds and whites, hearts, and flowers all around. I sat in the cosy restaurant, taking in the decorations and beautiful lights, feeling rather light-hearted.

Watching him from across the table as he sipped on his drink, I waited for the waiter to serve the meal we had ordered. He had a twinkle in his eyes, a twinkle that had been missing for quite a while.

'Release me from this suspense, please,' I entreated.

His lips twitched as he tried to stop himself from laughing. I could see he was enjoying making me wait and wonder.

'S.O., tell me now,' I cajoled.

'You guess,' he replied.

'Okay...,' I began. 'You got a job?'

'Yes.' His eyes seemed to gleam brighter. 'You're right in a way, but that's not the good part,' he said, smiling widely.

'See this man oh! Tell me *abeg*.' I was losing my patience.

Making a grand gesture out of it, he reached across the table and took my hand, then he said, 'I got a job abroad. We're going abroad.'

I sprang to my feet, screaming and flailing my arms. The other diners at the restaurant seemed alarmed at the outburst. My husband tried to get me to calm down, but I was too excited to notice anyone else.

Finally, I calmed down. He was so embarrassed that he had to apologize to other diners for disturbing the peace and tried to explain that he had just proposed.

Proposed? This was way better than when he proposed to me. But his explanation seemed to placate the disturbed diners and even elicited some 'congratulations' from them and indeed, the congratulations were well deserved.

When I had settled back down into my seat, I asked, 'How did it happen? Tell me.'

He explained that there was an opening in one of the branches of the organisation in Uzbekistan. They needed diversity in the company and he was at the right level for the position. It was a perfect fit and he was assigned the role.

I was beyond elated and thought, *This girl here has*

the boundary lines fallen for her in pleasant places. A job abroad! Are you kidding me? An expat assignment? Whooper!

The meal was served and we settled in to enjoy the catfish pepper soup before us. It tasted way better than I could remember. Everything tasted and felt better; I was on top of the world. But then who would not feel on top of the world given an international opportunity, a job with a full expatriate status in a reputable multinational? It was a big deal for us!

Soon after, we started making arrangements to leave the country. This was when it started to dawn on me that my identity, everything I had surrounded myself with for many years, might be taken away with no thought to how big a deal they were to me.

Home was going to be gone again, I was going to be exposed all over again and my insecurities would come to the surface again. Who is ever ready for this? I definitely wasn't, but we had to prepare for our new assignment.

First, I needed to resign from my job, hand over

properly and bow out. In my nine years there, I had climbed up the ladder to a comfortable position and had thoroughly enjoyed working with my colleagues. Back then, my department could not boast of having many female staff, so the few of us there were like jewels to our male counterparts. I enjoyed being the only *madam* in the office. I was doing great, and my boss was the kind of boss anyone could wish to have—a complete gentleman, professional, kind and good to work with.

Then, there was my small business with three employees looking up to me for their livelihood. Was I just going to let them down? I became aware of what I had built over the years and leaving them behind devastated me.

The distress became intense when my colleagues tried to remind me of how well I was doing and that I stood a good chance in the department. Besides, I had only just been promoted a few months back. It was a tough call.

As much as I love and was happy for my husband, I felt the pain of saying goodbye to the life I knew—

my comfort zone, if you like.

One day, my boss asked me into his office to consider my options carefully. He talked to me as a brother, not as a colleague. Hard as it was, I stood with my husband to go with him for the sake of my family and the home we had built over the years. 'I'm his wife and I will be where he is. After all, my name was to be Ruth,' was my response.

My boss then offered a bargain, 'Test run your new country, see if you like it. If not, you have a six-month window to come back to your job.'

Could anyone have asked for a better boss?

While I thought my boss was amazing and a father with a golden heart, my husband, on the other hand, saw it from a different perspective. He was stern and said my boss should stick to his official duties. He even promised to speak with him the next day. He wasn't impressed that my boss dared to suggest to me in the first instance that I might not like it. I explained to my husband that we have had colleagues in the past who went abroad and came back because they didn't like it there.

I was in a dilemma. There was a boss, trying to look

out for his esteemed officer and here was a husband who saw it differently. I pleaded with him to try and understand where my boss was coming from.

'You know the work-relationship we've had in the past. He's been a good boss by all means, although we do have our occasional rifts like during the summer school episodes, but he's only looking out for me,' I said to my husband. 'You can talk to him if you like. I just think that wouldn't be necessary,' I told him, trying to prevent an unpleasant confrontation between my loving husband and my great boss.

Finally, it was settled, and preparations began in earnest. A thousand and more matters had to be attended to. What would we need to take and what were we leaving behind for us to return to? Our assignment was supposed to be for three years. We decided to do some last-minute shopping and gave out most things, trusting that we would replenish them in Uzbekistan.

A few more nights and July came. Send-off parties were thrown here and there and soon, we were off. We were curious to know what life had for us in the new chapter of our lives. Come along with me to discover Uzbekistan for yourself and all the new realities I didn't even know existed.

POSTCARD FROM THE EXPAT'S WIFE

Before the move, do a cost-benefit analysis. Ask yourself what the relocation would cost you. Consider the losses and the gains.

For example, consider that you would be leaving your job and your support systems to venture into the unknown. Would you find new employment in the host location? Would your company provide support on housing, schooling and transportation, or would you have to handle these on your own? Would you need to learn a new language? How easy would it be to recreate a new support circle?

Be honest with yourself in doing this appraisal as that will get you ready for the challenges ahead.

In case your company provides support, then the agency will help you with documentation, housing, schooling and any other practical information you may need. If not, make the internet your best friend.

Chapter Two

OF SCREAMS AND SPECTACLES

'And suddenly you know it's time to start something new and trust the magic of new beginnings.'

~ Meister Ekhart

Passports, checked. Security, passed. Seat belts, fastened. Smiles, on. Aeroplane off the ground—away from my comfort zone.

My face beamed with joy in sharp contrast to my heart pounding with angst. A zillion thoughts overwhelmed my mind. My anxiety was nicely tucked beneath my playfulness with little Dami and Lizzie, my five and one-year-olds.

Oh! Travelling in an aeroplane was a different experience for my little children. It was fun for us all. For most of the flight, we sang nursery rhymes and threw our hands in the air. The children were so excited, they refused to sleep.

This was the era when you didn't have to fear any ugly incidence in the aeroplane—no shoe or pant bomb threats. I mean, I never gave a thought to the word *terrorism*, until a bit later. On this very day, all we were concerned about was flying high in the sky like eagles and feeling on top of the world.

We landed in Frankfurt after about six hours in the air. My husband joined us there as he had gone to Geneva, Switzerland for some training and we were soon on a connecting flight to our destination. We enjoyed the whole flight experience, the bumps, the cruise and finally, the children dozed off, and so did their Mama.

We were woken by the sudden announcement that we just landed in Tashkent, a city that would be our home for some time.

Uzbekistan is one of the 'stan' countries set in central Asia, a sibling of the other five: Kazakhstan, Tajikistan, Turkmenistan, Kyrgyzstan and Afghanistan. It is officially democratic with a diverse cultural heritage, as well as a member of the UN, Commonwealth of Independent States (CIS) and Organisation for Security and Cooperation in Europe (OSCE). Uzbek is the official language, although Russian is widely spoken because of the Soviet Union's influence in the country before its independence in 1991. Islamic religion is practised by majority of its people and the main source of the economy are commodity products such as gold, uranium, cotton, and natural gas.

If you were ever to visit or are simply curious about this country, this short history would be helpful. I too needed it before hitting the ground.

I was ready to feel the adventure as a first-time expat, ready to support my husband with his career and my children with their everyday needs. Most of all, I was ready to showcase Africa, shedding a positive light on a culture often misrepresented.

At Tashkent International Airport, we wobbled off the plane, proceeded with the immigration process, and eventually claimed our baggage.

Outside, a local Uzbek had been sent from my husband's office to welcome us. As I entered the cab, my excitement dissipated into terror at the thought of having no family and no friends around. Yet, for the sake of my reputation, I stayed strong and kept my fears to myself.

Glittering lights, beds of flowers, and too many policemen in clean-cut uniforms furnished the city. Not many souls were in sight. It was the middle of the night.

Once at the hotel, we were ready to test the softness of the Uzbek pillows. Inside our suite, silence bounced around as our weary bodies plopped on the white sheets and soon, two adults and two children snored away what was left of the night.

Morning came in the blink of an eye. As if on rapid count, the quietness of the night gave way to rumbustious hotel activities — a vacuum buzzing next door, the elevator's dinging sound, chattering voices heading to breakfast and my husband gently announcing his departure to work.

'What do we do, S.O.?' I asked him.

'Go to the restaurant and have breakfast. I will meet you up for lunch,' he whispered and took off.

'Okay.' That was all I could say.

I was in a four-star hotel. My first. And I didn't know

what to do with it. If there was an award for The Most Clueless Lady, I would have won it.

Clueless or not, breakfast had to be eaten because growling tummies looked up to me once they were awake. Not knowing what type of food to expect, I hurried to the menu placed on the desk in our hotel suite. It only took a second to know that we had to say goodbye to yam and stew, and *moi moi* and *ogi*. New words like croissant and mushrooms, although written in English, were nothing more than letters crammed together for my children.

Not knowing how to maze my way to the restaurant with two children, I opted for room service. The man on the other side of the phone whom I thought spoke English gave me more headache with a torturous English vocabulary fused with heavy Russian accent.

How hard is it to place my order? I asked myself. I wanted one omelette for myself, boiled eggs for my children, bananas, yoghurt, bread and to entertain my curiosity, croissants for all of us. After a tiring exchange of words, we were pleased to wait for our order.

Before morning ended, there was a knock on our

door. A serviceman whose English was limited to 'yes, yes' showed up with yoghurt, bread, bananas, croissants and an egg tray containing twelve boiled eggs (as if counting the twelve days of Christmas).

'Twelve boiled eggs, sir? I didn't order that!" I explained.

He shrugged his shoulders.

'Do you speak English, sir? I ordered an omelette and four boiled eggs for my children, not twelve. Do you understand?' I enunciated my disappointment.

'Yes, yes' was all he had to comfort my bewilderment.

Seeing that the conversation was going nowhere, I thanked him and shut the door after him. I've been trained to give thanks in all situations, whether in hunger or with a basket full of boiled eggs. We devoured the yoghurt, the plantain-like bananas, the delicious croissants and a few boiled eggs. The rest, we graciously left for my husband to enjoy when he returned for his lunch break.

The hotel was fully equipped with a pool, a gym, a restaurant, and a playground. My children desired to run wildly in the garden they had spotted out the window. We entered the elevator to see what fun we could find and were soon on our eager way down.

On the third floor, the doors squeaked open, and a lady stepped forward to enter. Then, she looked up and stepped back, shrieking as if she had seen a ghost. I wondered, genuinely concerned, if she was in danger as she turned and raced toward the stairs. The doors closed and the elevator continued its descent.

Once on the ground floor, I ushered the children out the elevator and hurried to the front desk. I told the clerk there about the incident, but the lady only smiled. I didn't think it was funny. Not sure I had made myself clear, I made a fresh attempt to tell her what happened. Just as I was doing so, the screaming lady made it safely down the stairs only to take another glance at us and scream some more.

It could have made for a funny movie, but for me and my children, it was terrifying. We all clung together in confusion.

The front-desk clerk reassured me that the lady was well and that this might have been her first encounter with black people.

Those words, 'black people.' I had never been described that way before. It was my first experience being *black*. The receptionist apologised and asked if she could be of any further assistance. I was too stupefied to say anything, I had nothing else to say or ask. I never expected to be so terrifying to another human being.

This encounter ruined the plans for the day. The children and I trudged up back to the fifth floor and I secluded all of us in the room like nuns in an abbey. My son was sorely disappointed. As for me, I couldn't stop thinking: *How will I ever develop friendships if I spook those around me?*

My husband came during lunch as he had promised. As he flung the door open, shouts of joy filled the room. Mine was louder than the children's. The first thing he saw were the eggs on the table then he said, 'Ah! Are you planning to start an egg business?'

It was the perfect opportunity to rant out our ordeal to him. He listened, then smiled. It was all he could do. Being more familiar with Uzbek culture than I, he vouched that this was a mere coincidence and not the norm.

***

Soon, the time came to move into our new home. Although the hotel hosted us for only five days, it felt like five months. Those first few days were bumpier than our plane ride.

The house was situated on Shivli Street 51. It was fully furnished and lacked nothing—a two-bedroom home with a fully equipped kitchen, a royal bathroom, and a sauna. The front yard also had a magnificent garden that had a gorgeous water fountain in its centre. The garden has a lush array of daffodils and roses.

I was grateful to the owner, thankful to God and pleased with my husband for providing us with such a beautiful, comfortable, spacious and luxurious home.

Just before we moved in, something funny happened. We discovered that the house was not burglar-proof. Since burglary proofing is a norm in my home country, we didn't realise that they do not do that overseas. Hence, the house was without the metal beams and protectors we were accustomed to. My husband? He said we would not take the house if those were not installed.

Note that at that period, it was difficult to get a good accommodation in Tashkent. The houses were not built with expatriates in mind because the country's economy had only just been opened to the rest of the world. People were only beginning to come in, so the houses were mostly for the locals alone.

As the country began to open up, few people began to build modern houses and the place we got was one of those. It was in this scarcity of modern houses that we got the house. Yet, my husband insisted that the landlord make the house burglar-proof if we were to move in.

The landlord replied, 'Why do I need to? It would make the house look ugly.'

I understood my husband's insistence. Being a frequent traveller, protecting his family in his absence was paramount. He said as much to the landlord, ending once again with his demand that the burglar-proof bars be fixed.

The man told him we didn't need it, but my

husband wouldn't take no for an answer. Finally, seeing that my husband wouldn't relent and because he really wanted us to take the house, the landlord conceded to put the burglar-proof bars on the doors and windows. So, we moved in.

Thankfully, all through our stay in Tashkent, there was no burglary incident.

It didn't take long to settle into our new home. The time finally came to get into the kitchen and make ourselves a simple stew for our boiled rice. Boiled rice, not boiled eggs. I had all I needed except onions. *Where could we find a market?* we wondered. We drove 'around the mulberry bush' without GPS, a city map or Russian language skills until we spotted a gentleman selling *shashlik*, which is grilled lamb skewers with sliced tomatoes and rings of onions. Onions!

We stepped out of the car and in minutes, the minuscule kiosk had turned into a tourist spot with a crowd competing with typical line-ups at the Eiffel Tower. It wasn't the *shashlik* that was drawing the crowds, it was our presence that had them flocking in like flies to honey.

My husband, following his business instinct,

grabbed two onions and swapped them for five dollars. The man's eyes lit up as if he had won the jackpot. With great sense of accomplishment, we made our way to the car, got in and drove home, sparing a backward glance at the curious crowd we had left behind.

That was not the only place we commanded attention. A good-sized Uzbek kindergarten neighboured our home. Locals passing by would pause on the driveway to see if they could catch glimpses of us stepping out of our home, either out of curiosity or a desire to get to know us. I hoped it was the latter. It was often very discomfiting, and we would sometimes return home to find strangers parked near our entrance, waiting to observe us. Even our driver turned into a local celebrity. If we spoke to anyone, they would become instant celebrities as other locals would bombard them with questions about us. On the bright side, my husband's barber got a lot more patronage because of us.

My son rather enjoyed the VIP attention. What five-year-old wouldn't?

I take pride in my children's good looks, and I thank my husband's handsome looks for them. At home, my family and friends used to pass them around like baskets of fresh bread. They were spoiled to bits. But things were different now as the Uzbek only asked to feel their skin and touch their hair. My son loved the spotlight, he'd push forward his five-year-old hand to shake theirs.

The touching was quite bothersome and so was their ignorance. One afternoon, I was tending to my flowers in front of my garden and a lady stood nearby. I wondered why she was standing in front of my house. She seemed uncertain, as if she wanted to say something but couldn't. Finally, she said hello to me, to which I responded.

Then struggling a bit with her English, she said, 'They don't wear clothes in your country...' Was that a question or a statement? I stopped what I was doing and smiled. Normally, I could have gotten angry at her statement, but I just looked at her and smiled. Then I asked, 'What's your name?'

'Aisha,' she said.

'Do you want to come in for tea?' I continued. She declined my invitation, promising to come the next day.

'Okay, I'll be waiting for you tomorrow,' I said. 'I would love to have tea with you.'

The following day, true to her word, Aisha came. But she didn't come alone, she brought a friend with her. I invited them in and when they were settled, I asked my help to make some *plov*, a local rice dish with lamb, to go along with the tea.

They seemed afraid but seeing one of their own in my home put them at ease. We ate and had our tea. Then I had the help bring my photo albums. There were two albums—my wedding album and another filled with general pictures. I handed my new friends the album, inviting them to feast their eyes on my pictures. She opened a page, looked at the picture and peered at me. She opened another page, studied the picture there and glanced at me again. Then she asked, 'This is you?'

And I said 'yes.'

Turning the pages, my new friends wowed at each picture. It was not what they expected. Little Kemi as a baby had colourful African dresses with her hair braided, smiling next to her happy parents. Nothing resembled the description they must have read in books about life in Africa. My wedding album wowed them the most. Most surprisingly, neither little Kemi nor her folks swung naked from tree to tree like monkeys.

When I was sure they had seen enough, I started, 'Now, I'm going to answer your question. You can see that we do wear clothes in my country.'

They all nodded in affirmation, Aisha looking particularly happy.

I had to educate them that Africa is a hub of civilisation, full of beautiful homes, grand art, rich culture, jaw-dropping scenery, perfect weather, and diverse animals in their free habitat that other countries caged in their zoos. Most of all, I let them know that Africa nestles friendly people with big hearts, not TV aliens.

From that day, Aisha became my ambassador, telling everybody about us. Suddenly, everyone wanted to be friends with us. They even corrected the gossip that my husband was the ambassador for Nigeria or the football coach for their national team. It's funny what people think up and spread in ignorance.

A simple photo album seen by two pairs of eyes

stopped the strange rumours in that community. Sadly, through this experience, I realised that African culture is disadvantaged by the media that portrays a culture that's strange to us.

More locals wanted to be friends with us, even though, initially, they were afraid and didn't know how to approach us. Uzbekistan was part of the former USSR, so they had been closed up with no television and no news other than what they were fed. As the country finally opened up, a lot of them were just getting to know the real world.

Aisha helped to spread the new narrative about the new Africa I told her about, to the extent that whenever the garbage collectors came for my garbage, they would come inside my compound to take it themselves. This was not their usual practice when I first arrived. They became my friends because of how Aisha spoke about us.

This experience taught me that there are biases in the world and the way to confront them is not by being angry or by protesting, but by a conscious effort of telling our stories to help outsiders know who we are. To let them see that Africa is not a country but a continent, and that Africa is not a jungle. And just like anywhere else in the world that I've travelled to, Africa has ghettos as well as amazing places. It's a battle we must keep fighting but not by physical warfare. We fight using stories.

By the way, my domestic help was my next-door neighbour. When we had newly moved in, she approached me to ask if she could help us with chores and such. She had worked for the former occupants of our new home and was available to help us, too. This arrangement was convenient for me as I could call from the fence, 'Mrs. Sabohats, could you help me do...?' and she would. Her husband was also available to help us anytime.

One Sunday, we drove down to explore the area and eight kilometres down the road, the police stopped us. Their English was non-existent, and our Russian was limited. We didn't know why we were pulled over. My husband handed them the necessary documents as more police officers appeared on the scene, but no one seemed to be able to communicate with us.

An hour later, a car pulled up alongside the road. As the man in a pristine uniform stepped out of the fancy ride, the crowd saluted him. He rushed toward us to shake our hands. Alas! Someone who understood what we were saying. After we answered a few questions and exchanged words and business cards, he informed us that no one would bother us anymore.

Finally, being different paid off. We were never stopped again by any police officer. We were treated with the utmost respect every time we encountered the police.

Part of my daily routine was to take my son to school and pick him up from school with the assistance of my driver. Dami loved every moment spent at the American International School. We allowed him to maximise his time enjoying the many available activities from music to gymnastics to language lessons and even to football (what they call soccer).

Each day when I went to pick him up after school, I would notice a little boy, not older than twelve, well-dressed with smiling eyes. The boy was Uzbek but his mum was Korean. As the heavy traffic often slowed our car in front of his house, he would wave until he couldn't see us anymore. Soon, another set of little hands joined him, fluttering hellos to us. Those hands belonged to his sister.

One day, I stopped the car to say hello. They spoke

no English. My *sposibo* and *privet* (thank you and hello) limited me to a smile and a wave. I looked to my driver for help. His English vocabulary, sadly, was limited to destination words such as school, market, and airport. I was left with the option of using my arms and feet if I wanted to forge this new friendship.

I looked to their mum and flailed my arms, asking for permission for her two children to join us that day. She nodded a yes and waved us to go. Once at our home, we exchanged lots of smiles over meals and playtime as the four children bonded.

Chris, my son's new friend, started to improve his English. Where the language seemed to limit them, the play, food, and laughter freed them from any boundary. Separated by distinct mother tongues, yet attached; unalike skin colours, yet unjudging; Africans and Uzbeks, yet united by love. What a joy it was to see my son learn to love those different from him.

Whenever I recall those years, I remember the inspiring words of Nelson Mandela: 'No one is born hating another person because of the colour of his or her skin, his/her background, or his religion. People must learn to hate, and if they can learn to hate, they can also be taught to love, for love comes more naturally to the human heart than its opposite.'

From my son's friendship with Chris, I learned that our minds are capable of loving beyond boundaries and that we're not different; we just have varied shades and colours. Sadly, we had to leave Uzbekistan before Chris excelled in English or we in Russian. We never had the chance to fully engage in a proper conversation. He will always have a special place in our hearts.

I wish my life was fuller with people like Chris with smiling eyes, waving hands and an energetic attitude. That's how I choose to embody the Uzbek, refusing the portrayal of the screaming lady on day one.

***

Uzbekistan takes pride in their open markets, from home decors to fresh veggies. Alayskiy Bazaar, our favourite one, delighted us with familiar foods like beans, semolina, rice, cow legs and tripe displayed on the vendors' stands. They even sold our precious onions.

All items were at a bargain price or so I thought. I was a foreigner as was my passport and money. Mesmerised by the vendors' kindness, more often than not, I would end up shopping for more things than I needed at a higher price.

I got a wakeup call the day my Russian teacher forced me to practice my new language skills at the market. That was when I knew that I had been paying as much as fifty Uzbekistan Sums for an item that cost five Sums in their local currency.

What could I do? I didn't know whether to laugh or cry. I learned to celebrate God's grace in spite of everything.

Life away from home had its aches—limited friendships, broken communication, cultural boundaries and unfamiliar cuisine, but what brought me more headache was the lack of my kind of shampoo. My head pounded daily with pain as I struggled to comb my natural hair. No boutique, supermarket, shop or hair salon in Tashkent sold the shampoo and moisturiser my hair needed.

One day, I braced myself to go to the professionals at the local beauty parlour. After using all my

Russian 'please' and 'thank yous' once again, I sat down. With my hands, I motioned to the hairdresser, trying to explain what I needed done to my hair.

She stared at me for a while and I stared back, then as if she understood my request, she began working on my hair. She washed and trimmed it a bit—an entangling experience for her scissors. When it was time to blow-dry my wet hair, the hair dryer blew more smoke than dry air, sending her clients out the door choking and coughing. I had to ask her to stop before we would have to call the fire department to rescue us from my hair disaster. Then I paid her and left, never to return.

My hair situation compelled even my husband to start feeling sorry for me. Not long after, he travelled to Moscow on a business trip. Moscow is the capital of Russia; it's bigger than Uzbekistan and had more black people and businesses. There, he met a gentleman working at the Nigerian embassy and asked him where he could purchase African hair products and food items.

Immediately, the man called his wife. She was the shopping expert. She asked them to come home and my husband went home with him. On reaching their home, she informed him that the market would have closed for the day but that she had a few things she could pack for me. She suggested that when next he came, they could go to the market together.

She was truly magnanimous. She packaged some hair products as well as dried *ogbono*, fish, grounded pepper and other items for him to bring to me. I was so excited when I saw the package. Two weeks later, I travelled to Moscow to meet her myself.

From Tashkent to Moscow is about four hours by flight, so it's not next door. I flew there to have my hair done and to buy some home supplies. I got there on a cold October day.

The kind lady picked me up at the hotel, took me shopping and even threw a party in her home, giving me the chance to meet more Nigerians. Oh, how I gulped down the homemade *amala* and *ewedu*. Laughter and joy replenished me well before I went back to Tashkent. I must have stayed in Moscow for about two days to do all of those before I flew back.

That woman was an angel, but we never kept in

touch because shortly after, we left for the Christmas holiday in Nigeria. At that time, we didn't have any technology such as cell phones to help us stay in touch.

***

My daughter Lizzie turned two and it was time to enrol her for preschool, a thought that scared me so much.

Since our arrival, she had been my constant companion when my son went to school and my husband to work. Out of fear, I pleaded with my husband to let me go back to Nigeria with our children. He denied my request. He needed us and I quickly realised that I can't quit supporting my spouse just because it's tough.

Lizzie was soon enrolled in the most popular English-speaking preschool in the neighbourhood known as Sunshine International.

With her not being there to keep me busy anymore, I realised I needed to find a way to stay active, so as not to lose my sanity. As if to reinforce my thoughts, I was introduced to an experience that scared me—*palpitations.*

How did it happen?

Since our move from Nigeria to Tashkent, I had lived a sedentary life. After a while, I began to notice that my heartbeat was sometimes irregular and out of tune. One day, it was so bad that I thought I was having a heart attack. My husband was not at home, so I went alone to the hospital to see a doctor.

The doctor knew me. Who wouldn't know the only black family in town? We were popular wherever we went.

'What happened, Mrs. Oloidi?' she asked.

'I think I'm having a heart attack!' I told her.

She examined me and sent me for an ECG to find out what was wrong. After the tests, she couldn't see any sign of a heart attack.

At this point, I had to explain what I was feeling to her. She told me it was not what I feared and advised that I needed to move and exercise because I had been passive for a long time.

It was true. I had started to gain weight. I knew for a fact that after having my two children I had remained a size six, but my recently sedentary lifestyle had begun to tell on me because in a short time, I had rapidly increased to size eight, then ten and more.

Back in Nigeria, I had had a full-time job that kept me busy. Here in Tashkent, I had helpers for almost everything, including the housecleaning and ironing. I wasn't active enough. I was eating a lot, gaining weight, and not exercising. There was a gym in the neighbourhood, but I couldn't go there because people stared a lot. They would even want to touch me, and I couldn't handle it, so I didn't bother.

I yearned to be among people so I decided to ask if I could volunteer at the school, but they turned me down because they said they had enough hands already. A few weeks later, they offered me a position as a kindergarten teacher. It was a 'praise God' moment that opened the door to a new experience among other expats and some affluent locals.

I was very happy about the new job because it kept me busy. Two months after I got it, the director of the school had to resign. Her husband had been posted to another country by his organisation, so she handed the directorship to me. This time, I was paid for my services.

As director, I handled the school's finances, took care of staff and taught the children in preschool. Children had to be six years old to start grade one hence, all children below six were enrolled in preschool until they came of age. I taught them multiplication, addition, and even did music time with them. I was super busy.

Nine months into our stay, we found an international church. Uzbekistan is an Islamic state, so it was uncommon to be a Christian there. How did I find the church? One afternoon while I was working in the school, I saw an Easter retreat sign on our notice board and I wondered, *Easter retreat here? Whoever posted this must be a Christian.*

I asked and was told it was one of the parents. Eagerly, I waited to speak with her and when we did, she was happy to know that I'm Christian too. She told me where the church was — the British Council.

On Sunday morning, we dressed up and went to the British Embassy. There was no church there.

My husband asked if I had heard correctly — was it the British Council or Embassy? I didn't know the difference, so I responded that it might be the British Council. We turned and went to the British Council. We arrived there when they were just closing the service.

I made new friends at the International Church. The pastor and his family were Americans, and we met each Sunday in the consulate. In God's sweet timing, He even uncovered for us a new friend from Nigeria who was married into the culture. I felt alive again after learning the lesson that God has His people everywhere ready for us to connect with, if only we use a tad of creativity and courage to press forth.

One of the downsides of living abroad is that it can be a lonely experience without friends. To keep your sanity, you have to look for people to connect with.

Like me, there were women who had come with their expat husbands and men who had come with their expat wives. I tried to connect with members of this group, especially when I started working in the preschool. I met other mothers in the preschool, and we became friends. I even made local friends because in Uzbekistan we were like rock stars—the black family everybody knew and wanted to be friends with. We picked a day in a week to meet either for coffee or lunch, and we would take our children along so that they could play together.

In a lot of ways, I missed out on a lot of opportunities to enjoy Uzbekistan. The money was there for any adventure I wanted because my husband's company gave him allowance to splurge on rest and relaxation, but Kemi never took advantage of such blessings. It was my first time out of Nigeria; I was timid and afraid.

I couldn't do a lot without my husband, and he was often away. I kept waiting for him but every day when he got home, he would say, 'Don't worry, don't worry, we'll do it this weekend.' The weekend would come meeting him tired and needing to catch up on some rest and sleep.

Many times, he urged me to go with the children just like the white women who had fun without their husbands. Those women were already exposed. As for me, I felt that I wouldn't know how to book myself into a hotel room with the children, so I never did it. I clung to my husband all through our stay there and we did not do much.

On one occasion, I shared with him my desire to visit England, Italy, Netherlands, USA, and Germany. He graciously took me to these countries before we left Uzbekistan but those were my ultimate. I could now say, 'I shopped in Paris, I ate pizza in Rome, I rehashed history by the walls of Berlin, I had scones and tea in London, and I walked the bridges of Amsterdam.'[1] At the time, I hadn't visited France though. That came later.

Still, the snow of God's creation topped them all.

It was October when I found them — a movie-like scene unveiled only inches away. I stayed glued to the window watching ash-like flakes swing gently from the skies. Not wanting to miss out on this wonder, I bundled up my children and scurried outside to touch those crisp flakes that inspire authors.

Despite the beautiful and white winter, we didn't spend any Christmas in Uzbekistan. By October of that first year, I was completely homesick and just wanted to leave, so I started pestering my husband.

[1]Quote from a book I do not remember at this time

As much as I was trying my best to adjust, there were still some things I couldn't handle. I still couldn't find the type of food we were used to. There was no plantain for dodo, no beans (and I love beans). I found black-eyed peas but that was not the variety I knew and liked, although I managed with that. I found something like semolina but other than that, there was no *ewedu* or *amala*.

True, I had some things shipped over but those things didn't arrive until very late and that was because Nigeria didn't have a bilateral agreement with Uzbekistan. Even making phone calls was difficult, you had to go to the telephone station to make calls to Nigeria.

All of these put together made me homesick and nothing would keep me back. The company was generous with a home leave provision that allowed their expats to go back to their countries as they wished. We took advantage of that and spent that Christmas and the next in Nigeria.

Because of our posting in Uzbekistan, God graced us to travel beyond my expectations. He helped us redefine what a quality family vacation should look like. Coming from a culture with the slogan 'hard work is the antidote to poverty,' I didn't know the refreshing value of rest.

In all, I can confidently say that despite all the cravings for our African dishes like plantains, *garri*, *elubo*, *egusi* and more, we never lacked in Uzbekistan. Not one day went by when Jesus didn't provide for us, plus He never said we would always have plantains.

***

All good adventures have an end. And so did our time in Tashkent.

It was time to pack. Again. Three more months and we would be off to our next assignment. Our hearts swelled with happiness.

Calling home was difficult, almost impossible at times and we were scheduled for our phone call at the telephone office. We loaded the car and drove off to reconnect with our family in Nigeria via the telephone. After a short ride, we parked. Dami and Lizzie moved towards the metal-framed door of the greyish building, thrilled to be out of the house and excited to talk to their grandpa, Baba Pastor, and his wife whom we all called Mama.

Calling our family was like a childish game of phone tag. We would give the phone officer the phone number we desired to reach in Nigeria. They would dial it and upon reaching someone, the call would be connected to us in one of their phone booths. We were all acquainted with the drill.

That day, the phone officer rang my husband's family in Nigeria as usual. Nothing seemed different until my husband's cheerful hello turned into a frantic 'What's wrong'? His voice weakened with each whisper coming from the other end. Leaning my ear close to his, I tried to make sense of the situation. I could hear a sob, followed by more sobs. My knees buckled beneath my skirt. The room became still. I could only hear the drumbeat of my heart, not knowing what had happened.

'Hello! Hello?' My husband insisted. 'Can you hear me? What happened? Hello!'

'Bose died,' a trembling voice on the other end of the line announced.

The brief conversation was disrupted by an untimely beep. The phone call ended, just like Bose's life. Bose was my husband's younger sister.

A rough season began for my husband. Although we were thirty days away from leaving Uzbekistan, he needed to be with his family *now*, so we packed faster and left earlier for our annual leave in Nigeria. We hoped that a thirty-day visit among family would be refreshing for us all.

It was a perfect plan. Thirty days was also the expected time to have our visas processed to move to our next place of assignment.

When the time came to go, we closed our chapter in Uzbekistan with goodbye parties and exchanged 'remember-me' gifts.

In Tashkent, I forged forever friendships and a closer relationship with my husband. Most of all, I left with an unforgettable lesson: fear can either cripple you and steal your joy, or it can kick you out of your comfort zone and help you grow. In my case, I grew.

POSTCARD FROM THE EXPAT'S WIFE

Before the move, consider your family.

Ask yourself, 'Is every member of the family on board the decision to relocate?' You must consider the children and their feelings before taking the final decision. Get their opinions. It wouldn't be easy for them to leave their friends and familiar places behind. Also, involve them in decisions concerning schools and housing.

Encourage and support one another. Talk to one another to alleviate any fear or concern each family member may have and reassure them that you are there for them.

Chapter Three

IN NATURE'S CRADLE

'Travel early and travel often. Live abroad, if you can. Understand cultures other than your own. As your understanding of other cultures increases, your understanding of yourself and your own culture will increase exponentially.'

~ Tom Freston

It is well known that a travelling Nigerian always starts his journey well ahead of time, with an exaggerated amount of paperwork for visas, work permits, medical requirements, school submissions and everything in-between.

Before departing Uzbekistan, we had submitted our stack of papers at the embassy in Moscow, but at that same time, the Kenyan government had amended and placed more restrictions on entry requirements into their country. That we were sons and daughters of the same soil made no difference.

I was still glad we were heading to Africa. Its name is like a kaleidoscope of meanings: afar meaning dust, afri is *a tribe* in North Africa; then the Greek *Αφρική* (pronounced aphrike) meaning *without cold* or the Latin word *apica* meaning *sunny*.[2] To me, Africa only meant home.

My sweet home, where all would be familiar again — the smells, the tastes, the unconventional ways of doing things, the hustle and bustle of big cities, the rain, the heat, the resilience of the black person... all of it.

It would feel good to not stand out anymore, to not use my hands and feet to speak a foreign language, and to not have a white woman scream in the elevator. Being back among similar-skinned people, we would be a perfect blend. No more culture shock, or so I thought.

Family time in Nigeria benefitted us greatly but we were soon ready to fall into a routine and settle into the expat life again. We could not go back to Uzbekistan since we had chosen to leave early due to the family emergency neither could we go to Kenya because our visa status was taking longer than expected. We had no option but to stay in Nigeria and soon, our thirty-day visit turned into a

[2]https://www.sheppardsoftware.com/Africaweb/factfile/africauniquefact5

hundred and eighty days. Our choices had put us in a pickle.

After staying in a hotel for a month, I told my husband we couldn't stay there anymore, so we rented an apartment in Ikeja and enrolled Dami and Lizzie at Chrisland School.

Back then, Nigerian landlords often demanded three years' advance payment. However, our landlord was kind. When we told him that we were in transit but needed the house, he promised that whenever we moved, he would refund the money. Our humble dwelling was small and poorly furnished. All our belongings were on their way to Kenya even though we weren't.

We had a bit of savings when we left Uzbekistan but ran into a little financial difficulty because of our home building project.

Before we got back to Nigeria, we had had people assisting with the project but because we were home, we thought it was the right opportunity to complete it since we didn't know when our visas would connect. This family project consumed our time, owned our to-do list, drained our energy, and depleted our savings. Bad timing.

The Uzbek office wouldn't pay my husband any longer. The Kenyan office couldn't pay him yet. The Nigerian office didn't even recognise him since he was in transit. No salary. No income. A journey in the wilderness that dried our pockets and our emotions.

We rushed everything and were able to get the house to a reasonable stage. In every other aspect of our living, we were careful with spending.

As our money shrunk, a lot of people we thought we could count on left us. My people have a saying: 'Close your eyes and pretend to be blind, see who will mock you. Pretend to be dead and see who will mourn you.' When we found ourselves in that situation, a lot of people abandoned us like they couldn't be bothered. I kept wondering why it was like that. Much later, some said they were not aware of our situation while some said they thought we were joking.

When everyone else deserted us, my uncle stood by us. I cannot forget the amazing thing that happened on Christmas Eve. He came to my house and was surprised that we were not preparing to celebrate Christmas. I told him we didn't have money for Christmas, so it would be just another normal day for us. He went out and returned with chicken and snacks for my children so that they wouldn't miss out on Christmas. Everybody was happy.

My uncle will always remain my husband's hero. A lot of people who don't know our story often wonder why my husband likes my uncle specially. This is the story. My uncle was there when no one else was.

During this financial crisis, God gave us a three-fold gift of enjoying quality family time, sifting real friendships, and leaning on Him like we never had before. Prayer became our favourite pastime. Having plenty of time on our hands, we immersed ourselves in ministry. It was convenient since we lived at a spitting distance from the church.

As the months dragged by, I battled with the what ifs. *What if it was a wrong decision to move early out of Uzbekistan? What if we needed to move in with family? What if...*

I wallowed in self-pity, burdened with the guilt and uncertainty of our decisions. We had no choice but to take it one day at a time as we had no timeline of how much longer things would have to stay this way.

After six months in Nigeria, our papers were ready for us to move to our new home, but I was not. I allowed my fears and exhaustion to speak for me.

My little ones were adjusting to their new school, building new friendships, and bonding with their new teachers. Why uproot something barely planted, stealing from them the right to bloom? I reasoned. I was also back into my routine of a hustling African mother and wife.

I begged my husband to leave the children and me behind a little longer for stability's sake, but he refused. The back-and-forth pleadings were déjà vu of Uzbek's pre-relocation experience. Same sentences, different geographical location.

Family is so important to both of us. It is the value that brought us together in the first place. Having somewhere to go is home, having someone to love is family, and having both is a blessing. For both of us, loving and being loved was not just important, it was everything.

I yearned to have Ruth's dedication, but my heart was not ready to echo her words: 'Wherever you go, I will go, and wherever you live, I will live; your people will be my people and your God will be my God.'

I expected my mother to support my choice, but her bluntness made me angry. She spoke the truth, although it did not sit well with me. 'Come sun or rain,' she said, 'unless the relationship is life-threatening, a woman must stick by her husband. Go to Kenya.'

I heeded her words, and off we went.

***

The sun was ready to launch the day as we touched down in Nairobi, Kenya. A bright morning filled with bright smiles throughout the airport. Flight attendants neatly lined up in their bright red uniforms greeting incoming passengers.

No other airport welcomed us like this one. I felt special but it had nothing to do with us. Airport staff and flight crews were commemorating the tragic Flight 431 off the coast of Cote d'Ivoire earlier that year.

A Kenyan woman came to receive us. My husband's office had sent her to guide us on our first day. She made a stunning first impression, a slender and stylish woman in a pencilled yellow skirt, army-green top, hair held back in an elegant ponytail, carrying a leather handbag. Kenyan women have a way with colours, they combine the oddest nuances to create style.

Once settled in the hotel, we were ready to eat. Unlike our previous experience in Uzbekistan, we didn't order a crate of boiled eggs. Instead, we hastened toward breakfast, unbothered about how it would taste.

To my surprise, the hotel hosted lots of white folks. I felt as if I was not in Africa. Kenya was home to a lot of businesses and major international companies. Hotel staff were well-equipped to deal with adults and children alike. They high fived my children as they assisted them on the playground and offered to do painting, colouring, and lots more.

Kenya had already won my heart. Its capital, Nairobi, was a vibrant city with a beautiful mix of whites, blacks and other races, especially Indians. They were mostly well-cultured people. I fell in love with Nairobi, the largest city in the country which was named after the river floating about the city.

Most people in the city wore jeans and t-shirts but I loved the Maasai — the colourful indigenous costumes tightly wrapped around their slender bodies, and their big ear lobes decked with humongous earrings.

Before long, we unlocked the door to our new home, a fully furnished apartment on Riverside Drive, a luxurious part of the town. Every piece in the home was modern and artistic. Our compound was surrounded by green space, and the safe and quiet neighbourhood allowed us to go for brisk walks in the mornings.

Our apartment had it all, including a backup power supply in case there was a power outage, which was common at the time due to the drought problem in East Africa. During that period, electricity had to be rationed such that the commercial areas had electricity from 0600 hours to 1800 hours and 1800 hours to 0700 hours for the residential areas. This situation lasted for six months.

Dami and Lizzie adjusted faster than my husband and me. They were every parent's dream — no tantrum fits and no health problems. They interacted with children and adults with ease. We enrolled them in the Braeburn School in Nairobi. It was different from their former American school, but it had a perfect blend of excellent teachers, assistants, and little friends.

The British curriculum-based school invited the parents to a lot of extracurricular activities — Diwali Day, Guy Fox Day, music festivals, sports festivals, swimming competitions, recitals, soccer games and much more.

My children grew in wisdom and stature in Kenya. Dami's highlight was winning a swimming prize. For Lizzie, it was getting a standing ovation on Fashion Day as we set her on the podium to showcase her catwalk talent, dressed in our Yoruba native attire and headgear[3] and her face flourished with befitting makeup. Amazingly, she still is a *fashionista* currently writing her fashion blog and managing an online beauty magazine she founded.

We knew no boredom in Kenya. There was not enough daylight to keep up with our new life's demands between school, church, and neighbourhood.

Life here was a total contrast to that in Uzbekistan.

[3]*Indigenously known as iro, buba and iwaju layewa*

This time around, I grabbed the opportunity to live life to the full. I made a lot of Nigerian friends, and we went out a lot and had good times.

The only issue was that we still didn't have Nigerian foods. Kenyans eat like white people; one could only get Nigerian food when somebody travelled home and that was how we got ours. Each time one of us travelled to Nigeria, they would bring *garri*, yam and other foodstuffs to share with us. Some of them bought stuff from Dubai to resell to us. There was a lady who made local delicacies. If one was craving a particular meal and told her they wanted that meal, Biola would prepare it and sell it to them.

We lived and did things together and as most of us were Yoruba, we had our *owambe* regularly. Every weekend, there was one event or the other, from children's birthday parties to adult events. That was how we kept ourselves busy.

I didn't want to take up a regular job as the pay was next to nothing, but I did some buying and selling. Some Nigerian ladies would travel home and return with *kampala* fabrics and other unique clothing materials one couldn't find in Kenya. I would purchase fabrics from them and resell to Kenyans within my circle; these were in demand because they fell in love with our Nigerian fashion for weddings and other special occasions. After some time, I stopped selling those because they were not meeting up with payments.

One thing that made Kenya a joyful place to live was friendship.

My husband loved holding his huge Yoruba Bible whenever we came to church. It paid off in more ways than we expected. One day while we were at the Nairobi Pentecostal Church, Mr. Folami, a strong man of faith, intrigued at the sight of his Bible, came to greet us. In no time, we found ourselves sharing dinner at their kitchen table, delighting in Mrs. Folami's delicious recipes. It was the start of a long-lasting relationship.

I also joined a Bible study that met weekly at a Baptist church. We each took turns hosting the group. People gathered from many countries as we will in heaven.

My eight-year-old son gave his life to Jesus in Kenya. He was soon reading his Bible and asking questions. Every evening, we would hold faith discussions. To the glory of God, both my children are following Christ to this day.

> *'Train up a child in the way he should go: And when he is old, he will not depart from it.'* Proverbs 22:6 (King James Version)

***

Kenyan food was delicious, but it lacked the chillies Nigerians, especially Yorubas, thrive on. Moreover, my family didn't share in my love for *sukuma wiki* and *ugali* but we all adored their fresh plantains and jointly disliked their hard tasteless yam.

I got most of my food, souvenirs, decorations, and cleaning supplies at the city market or the Uchumi supermarket. Everything was available at a reasonable price, although the city market was quite a handful for tourists and newbies due to the locals upping their prices as they pleased.

My favourite place was Gikomba. It was the largest fish market, a place not for the faint of heart — or nose. The scarce pockets of fresh air due to the pungent fish smells, the nerve-wracking pickpocketing, the glue-sniffers, the loudness, the chaos, the tension, and the too-many options of water creatures made for a dizzying experience.

The fish possibilities for dinner were endless; there was salmon, sniper, catfish, tilapia, red sniper, lobster, prawns—all could be fresh, dried, smoked, scaled off or cleaned at your request.

Evans, my driver, lived nearby. Since parking was almost impossible, we usually left the car at his house and walked to the market on foot. I inherited this love for fish from my grandmother, a brilliant fishmonger who taught me the difference between a good catch and stale bait.

The long drive was worth it each time. Love for fish was not the only attraction there, Gikomba also hosted the largest second-hand market. This was, and I presume it still is, a big market in Kenya. Kenyans patronise this second-hand market with pride. It's where one can get beautiful designer outfits for very pocket-friendly prices.

Say tourism and that was Kenya. 'No sleeping at the coast' was our slogan while taking a tour of

Mombasa, a slogan that travels with us even today.

A calm seashore contrasted with our lively hotel where there were themed entertainments, an abundance of food, adventurous safari rides and great people to glue them all together.

For the first time, I encountered wild animals in their natural habitat. They invaded my space too, with some monkeys entering our room through the open windows.

We toured Hell's Gate in Naivasha — a unique experience with no tour guides, allowing humanity to meander and mingle with zebras, tall spitting giraffes and large buffalos. The unbearable heat cut our trip short, causing us to miss out on climbing the hills and cliffs it hosted, making it less eventful than the intense name it bore.

While in Tashkent, we had missed out on a lot of opportunities to explore new places. Having learned our lesson, we took a family trip to Dubai for Christmas.

We arrived in Kenya in February 2000 and lived there for a year. Because we had stayed too long in

Nigeria, I didn't want to travel back for Christmas. Coupled with the experience of our friends turning away, I wasn't happy with a lot of people. We decided to visit Dubai since my husband was around and was able to take a two-week holiday.

Dubai was not as it is today. It was beautiful but life then was cheaper. Without many taxes, we bought a lot on our visit. We enjoyed our stay as it gave us a plethora of things to see and do from the spice and gold souk to affordable shopping and high-quality water activities. The Wild Wadi Waterpark gave us a scare though.

Another incident during that vacation scared me. I had been exhausted from all the fun on one of the days and decided to remain in one place while Lizzie wandered in the shallow pool. Taking my eyes from her for a moment, she waddled away into the deeper part of the water. She struggled for life until a lifeguard came to her rescue. I received a serious scolding from her rescuer.

It took Lizzie months before she could tiptoe in water pools again and it was only when we moved to Belgium that she resumed swimming and only because it was part of her school curriculum.

***

Kenya presented itself with great opportunities for the whole family — quality education, exciting getaways, deep friendships, a church community, and plenty of opportunities for growth.

I love children and when we got to Kenya, I wanted to go back to the university to study child psychology and thereafter start a childcare/day care business. I didn't get the chance because we weren't going to stay in Kenya long enough. But I told a friend about my desire, and she told me about a nanny training school for the locals, which, if completed and coupled with my education background would give me the leverage to start my own business.

She told me the person in charge was American and asked if I would like her to connect us. I agreed and she did. That was how I got to know Nancy.

Nancy and I met for coffee, and I told her why I wanted to do this. I went on to submit a formal application and after a formal interview, she enrolled me. After paying the fees, the classes commenced. It was a rigorous experience, especially the practical bits. It was a nine-month training where I got equipped and certified as a nanny to provide CPR, plan a balanced diet for children and handle large groups of babies and toddlers.

Still eager to further my education, I planned to enter the Kenya Institute of Developmental Studies, but that dream ended before it even began. Information from my husband's office reached us that he was no longer needed overseas. I grieved at the thought of going back home and giving up the expat life with all its unique blessings.

Prayer became my only outlet. Day and night I prayed, fasted, worshipped, and prayed some more. At times, expectantly and at other times, anxiously. Despite our smaller-than-mustard-faith, God answered and that summer, we were posted to Belgium.

Expats become experts at goodbye. Toward the end of our stay, we threw a garden party for our friends and colleagues. We did it the *owambe* style with colourfully intricate dresses, lively music, and international cuisine of puff puffs, jollof rice, fried rice, assorted meat and fish, ice cream and an abundance of store-bought cakes. The singing, dancing, sharing of food and laughter made for a joyful celebration of God's goodness for each day lived in Kenya.

POSTCARD FROM THE EXPAT'S WIFE

Before the move, plan how to survive the first few days of arrival in the new location.

What staple food items, medication and/or infant formula would you need to take along with you? How would you restock in the new location? Remember that younger children may not be able to adapt to changes immediately, especially with food. My son stayed hungry for some time and that was stressful for our family.

Sometimes, it may take time before you are able to leave your new host country, especially when your immigration documentation is in process, so make adequate plans for an extended stay.

Chapter Four

EUROPE MY LOVE

'For the Lord God is our sun and our shield. He gives us grace and glory. The Lord will withhold no good thing from those who do what is right.'

~ Psalm 84:11

Belgium was grey and damp with too much rain.

When we were transferred to Belgium, a lot of people asked why we wanted to go there and why we didn't choose England or even America. To be honest, my husband did try to change it to the UK because I have my sister there and they speak English, but the company had made their decision and that was it.

People tried to dissuade us further by recounting the rising rate of racism in Belgium. I was reminded of the weather, the history of slavery and the human zoo. The language was also going to be an impediment, and the culture and social life differed from what I was used to.

Everyone apart from my husband and my driver believed the Belgium assignment should be rejected and soon, the negativity got to me, and I became scared.

It took my driver's effort to yank me off my fears. He said to me, 'Madam, you're a good person. Don't worry, whether there's a problem there or not, God will protect you. You're a Christian, God will be with you. Don't worry about whatever anybody is saying, just make up your mind that you're going in God's hands and that He is leading you.'

That was my wake-up call, so I told my husband we would go to Belgium.

Since then, we never discuss our relocation with a third party until we are ready to move. We just tell them we have been transferred to avoid any discouragement from anybody. If God says we're to go into a hole, that's where we will go. We decided as a family that for the rest of our assignments and journeys in life, we would keep our businesses to ourselves.

Many people, even in good faith, will offer advice

based on their life experiences forgetting that our experiences will be different as would the outcomes.

As for my husband, he has always been determined and does well with handling challenges, plus he thrives in competition. He gloated at the opportunity to work in the European office and no amount of scepticism would stop him.

I entered Belgium with a lot of uncertainty. I didn't know what to expect. I had visited in the past and loved the vibes and atmosphere however, one would agree that visiting and residing in a place are two different experiences.

As usual, we stayed in the hotel for about a week to get our housing and documentation sorted out. The hotel was in the centre of Brussels, so it was easy to view the city as tourists.

The Grand Place was beautiful with thousands of tourists trooping from all over the world while the smell of Belgian waffles permeated the air. There was always one kind of open-air show or the other going on within its premises. Then some entertainers posed as statues covered from head to toe in silver or gold. I kept wondering what would happen if I touched or pinched one of them. Would they blink if I stared long enough?

I was tricked at first to believe that these statue-like entertainers were not humans because of their perfect poses. I wanted to pose with one of them for a photograph, which would have been a highlight for me. I wanted to be a child again and act naughty, but I let it pass as I was not ready for what could come after.

Restaurants were scattered around Grand Place and its environs. Notable for its fries and mussels, waffles and the 'Miss Me Not' Chocolat Chaud, vendors called out to tourists to come and have a taste of their food. Oh, the food!

I developed a good taste for fries, anything I ate must come with fries. It was a beautiful addiction for me, and I did not mind if it began to grow on my head (when I was young, some people would tease that certain foods would sprout from my head if I ate them too much). The chocolate drink was also my favourite. What's not to love about it? I drank so much that it became a part of my daily routine.

There are many monumental buildings in Belgium that adorned Brussels, such as the European

Parliament building, the Royal Palace, beautiful cathedrals, and monumental sites. This does not exclude the surrounding cities and towns — Woluwe with the shopping centre, Leuven with the oldest and biggest university in Belgium, the Gothic town hall, and the breath-taking architecture. There is Namur and the majestic citadel which is now a public park. I was told that it was once the most powerful stronghold in Europe.

After about a week in the hotel, I was tired of eating restaurant food and ready to move into a little semi-detached house we had rented in the city of Overijse.

Our new home was cosy and beautiful. During our look-and-see visit, I chose the house and made input on the interior design. The owners were good people; they agreed to all the changes that I requested without asking too many questions. However, we paid for the curtains and a few other things that were changed. Shortly, it became a home for my family and me.

The two-and-a-half bedrooms (one was a mini bedroom, in my opinion) with a sizable living room, dining room and private garden were all we needed. The kitchen was equipped with modern appliances and the private garden was well-maintained. The trees and flowers in the garden were well nourished. We loved the house and enjoyed spending time there with one another and a few friends.

***

Because we moved in the summer of that year, schools had closed and a lot of the other expats had gone back home for the long holiday. We met only a few people upon arrival.

Dami turned nine during this time and we threw a small birthday party for him. He wasn't particularly enthusiastic about this birthday, unlike the previous years when he would be so excited. He would ask me how many people he should invite over, what they were going to eat and what games to play. He would barely sleep the night before.

But this birthday was different. That day, he let us know that 'Having your birthday in a new country where you have no friend sucks!' Maybe we should have waited for him to have his party before we moved but excitement and curiosity got the better of us. Moving at the time we did wasn't a good decision for him.

There were only three children on our street; one of them was too young to be his friend and the other two didn't speak English. All we saw of them were of them leaving in the morning and coming back together or sometimes, separately in the afternoon. Anyway, I invited both of them to join us to celebrate my son's birthday.

They came with a small gift for the birthday boy, but my son saw them as strangers and that made it worse. He felt he could have enjoyed his day better with just the four of us than to spend it trying so hard to be friendly with people he didn't know or whose language he couldn't speak.

I thought children could play without having to necessarily speak the same language, after all, we discovered that with Chris in Uzbekistan. I asked him what was different; why was he able to play with Chris without any reservations but not these ones? He reminded me that he had grown older. Besides, it was not on his birthday that he met Chris. He had a point. I accepted both facts and apologised that we had moved before his birthday.

On the other hand, my daughter's fifth birthday was phenomenal because school had resumed by then. They had made friends from school and church, and many of her friends came for a sleepover before the actual day.

On D-day, we had so much fun. The cake was beautifully decorated with fruits. She dressed up in her native attire, looking gorgeous. We played games, including *dress up* where the children dressed up in Nigerian native attires. It was colourful and beautiful. We took pictures and my husband had them printed before the end of the party so that the children could take them home with them. Parents were impressed and ordered enlargements.

The area where we chose to live in Belgium was mostly populated by retired elderly people. A few of them were still working but I could count on my fingers how many of us were in the same age bracket and I had no idea why that was so.

Another thing I noticed was that the older people were well-off, with better cars and bigger houses. I asked and was told that the seniors are free from the burdens of a high tax rate and that their pension was also good.

We chose the suburban area because it felt safer there without the hustle and bustle of the city. It was calm and quiet, but one needed to have their car or a means of transportation otherwise, they were left with one option: the bus that runs hourly until 1800 hours.

Our neighbours were nice and friendly, except the one man that my children nicknamed Grumpy. He told me he doesn't like children and he wouldn't have them play in front of his house. He made sure I understood that if my children's football ended up on his property, they must say a final goodbye to that ball. I warned my children never to go near his house or kick their ball into his garden, but children would always be children. Even after my warnings, they let their ball get into his compound a couple of times but in fairness to him, he sometimes threw the ball back to them.

By and large, other than Mr Grumpy, all other neighbours were friendly and kind. They were always ready to help me. They gave information without reservation and eagerly offered their assistance whenever I needed one.

We occasionally had dinners with our neighbours, got invited to birthdays and in turn, invited others for barbeques as well. It was a community of friendly and kind people.

Louise, a French-Belgian lady, tall and slender, told me that her best days were the ones she and her family spent in Africa. Her family worked in Congo as diplomats, and she carried a very sweet memory of her time on my continent. Louise gave my son a school bag for his next birthday. She bought the famous Harry Potter book, one for each child. Another lady, widowed, who lived alone, would always bake and bring cake to us.

My children were blessed with a lot of grandmas in that community. I became very close to Rita, an elderly lady, the best of them all. She never gave up on me, even when we moved to another street in the same neighbourhood.

We did not experience the stereotypical behaviour we were told about in Belgium except on few occasions. This gives me the confidence to tell people that wherever we went, there was always another side to every story.

Belgians are kind-hearted people, regardless of what happened in the Dark Ages. With all that is happening in our world today, a cynical view about human nature can be easily formed. However, I have received generosity and kindness from different races and ethnicities to know better. So, I refuse to believe that evil has a monopoly over human nature. I would rather believe that goodness is alive and in all of us, it's just up to each of us to show the better side of our nature in the likeness and image of God.

I remember having a friend who was not very nice in most of her comments to me. As a friend, I took her to meetings or wherever we had to go together. On our way, she would always point to this place in Belgium where slaves used to be exhibited in Tervuren Centre. Every time she did this, she would laugh hysterically, asking me if I knew what they did in that place. One morning, I wasn't going to ignore it anymore so I parked my car and told her to get down if she would go on taunting me about such a despicable inhuman memory. She realised her mistake and apologised.

Though this was a nasty experience, it was not enough to tag the entire population with whom we had had more good experiences as racists. We cannot base our judgement about a whole country or continent on one encounter with one uninformed person. That would be similar to what they say about Nigerians being scammers. I am not one and neither is my husband.

Another attraction to the area we lived in was its nearness to an international church. My family and I always preferred living in places where we could find English-speaking churches. We enjoyed fellowshipping with other Christians and would always look for a home church — a Pentecostal church. That has always been one of our many anchors, a place of succour and friendship. We have always tried to mix with people so that we can do life together and help one another.

The church is where I always feel relevant and acceptable without any prejudice. It is where I met Sue, an American and a friend closer than a sister. I also met Cecilia from Papua, New Guinea. Oh, Cecilia! How I loved that woman! She was my walking buddy and we explored Overijse together. She even introduced me to my best physician. Another wonderful child of the Most High God was Maina from the Republic of Congo. Peter and Terrence are friends and family till tomorrow. I also met Celia, Tony and their children from South Africa. Celia taught me some South African cuisines. Now, I make biryani like a local and my tiramisu is the best, thanks to her. I also learnt a bit about home décor from Celia.

God is faithful to have given us godly influencers to

walk life with when family and friends were far away from us. We always had people to call and enjoy growing with. Tayo and Ngozi are still a backbone till Jesus comes. Even though we knew each other from Nigeria, we got closer in Belgium. To all these people, I say thank you for being there for us. God always provides for our needs according to His riches in Christ's glory.

Despite all the wonderful people that graced our lives in Belgium, I must confess that my first few years there were pretty hard. It took me three years to find my footing. I loved visiting Europe but not until I had to live there did I acknowledge some harsh realities, and they hit me badly.

Firstly, I couldn't really connect with the locals. They mostly stayed in their homes and minded their business. It was tough living through this experience. Their kind of social hangouts were quite different from mine.

Even though I got a job offer in a British school shortly after I got to Belgium, I couldn't get a work permit, so I had to work instead as a volunteer, helping in the classroom with the six-year-olds. I did this for six months and left because it was impacting my family in a way that was against my family ethics. Working there meant staying longer hours before picking up my children from school and dropping them off too early to be able to meet resumption time in my job. It meant getting home tired and barely able to do anything with my own children as much as I liked. My family and I decided it was okay to stop and I faced my primary duties of being a mum.

Another issue was the weather. It was always dark. The skies were constantly grey, and we seldom had blue skies. In Uzbekistan, the weather was great. They had their terrible winter, but summer was warm and nice like... summer. That was not the case in Belgium.

Here, there was no defined weather. In June, you could still be wearing your jackets when others were already enjoying the summer warmth. Everything was mixed — foggy, cold and windy, rainy and sunny at the same time.

Initially, I couldn't connect the weather with our wellbeing, but I soon began to notice that people tended to display a happier attitude whenever the sun smiled on us.

They say Nigerians are happy people. Thinking

about it now, I would say it's probably because of our sun. We don't appreciate what this sun is doing for us. I regard it as one of the reasons more people have not died of depression in Nigeria.

In those early years in Belgium, I didn't know the sun was affecting my mood. I would always have mood swings. At one point, I told my husband I didn't think I could cope. I was constantly afraid and anxious and would call him several times in the day just to know when he would be back home.

Depression is real! It didn't take too long for me to break down completely. That was when we realised I needed to see a doctor.

Before then, I didn't know what depression was. I come from Nigeria, had a great relationship with my family and my friends, and I was happy. What did depression have to do with me?

I started seeing a doctor and he placed me on medication. The medication helped to lighten my mood, but it made me gain so much weight that I couldn't go up the stairs. I was so big that my bones started to complain, and I had to rely on my husband to help me.

I soon became fed up and decided that I couldn't

continue with the medication. When I told the doctor about it, he told me it couldn't be stopped abruptly; I would need to wean myself. I couldn't wait for that long on a medication that I felt was killing me, so against the doctor's instructions, I stopped.

That was not a good move. I must firmly state here that no one should do what I did. Stopping a medication abruptly is very dangerous and I paid the price. Do not do it!

I must also add here that people often think and say that if one is a true and prayerful Christian, they cannot be depressed. This is not true. By the grace of God, I am a Christian. I prayed — I was leading the prayer ministry in my church — but I became depressed. That's not to doubt that prayer can help. Prayer helps because a lot of people prayed for me, and it went a long way. I didn't stay depressed for long.

A lot of people from my church really showed up for me during that phase. They came around, took me out, gave me nice treats and soon, I started to get better. I guess I was now getting the necessary attention that I was used to.

My therapist helped me, too. He was the one who told me, 'What you are not able to change, you find a way around it.' So much truth in one sentence.

I couldn't change the weather in Belgium, the best I could do was find a way to cope with it. That was a big lesson for me. I realised that no situation can break you without your permission and if you will persevere, you can get over it. And that's what happened to me. Once I acknowledged that I had to find a way to cope, I began to love Belgium. I got engaged in many other social and Christian activities and became alive again.

During that period, my friend Sue Shook and I made a decision together to never be bored. I embraced the International Christian Women's Club. There I met other interesting and lively ladies: Sandra, Celia and many others who love the Lord and are happy to help others love Him. I enjoyed what we did as board members of the ladies' club. Boredom and idleness soon left my life and life became enjoyable.

***

The weather and all that came with it wasn't the only experience that shook me in Belgium. So many things presented as difficult in the beginning. Sometimes, the smaller things in life are those that threaten to trip one up. One of such seemingly small things was the matter of garbage disposal — the recycling business.

I found the recycling culture in Belgium rather perplexing initially. I was confused about everything. The collection days were different to start with, and I couldn't determine what went into which coloured bag. Since I left my country of origin, Belgium was the third country that I had lived in, and I had never in the past concerned myself with what happened to garbage. I had house staff who saw to that. But this was not the case in Belgium.

In Belgium, we didn't have the luxury of hiring a maid. I steered clear of acting as the boss lady because the process of hiring one was not only cumbersome but also very expensive.

This meant that I had to concern myself with matters pertaining to tackling trash. It was a mess! I would often take out the wrong bag on the wrong days. I got to understand my errors the hard way when my garbage was not picked up for weeks. Thanks to a neighbour, I finally learned the ropes of the Belgian garbage disposal system.

I realised that I had to separate garbage into different bags, ensuring that the cans and bottles were clean before putting them in their designated bags. This meant that before discarding, for example, a can of orange juice, I had to first rinse the can, otherwise it would attract a fine after three warnings. It was a big culture shock for me. That day, after the clarification, I had to take the bags back inside until the next day. The rottenness and the stench were unbearable.

Another thing that was unbearable to think about was the thought of buying the disposal bags. I found that buying the bags for discarding waste with was a 'capital project' that needed a separate budget.

Talking about budgets, I found things in Belgium to be more expensive than I was used to. The cost of everything, even the recycled wastewater, was on the high side. The bills were unending, and nothing came free. Taxes were high, electricity and the cost of heating the house was exorbitant for us. We were used to living lavishly but moving to Belgium taught us a good lesson in managing our resources.

This memoir wouldn't be complete without an account of my driving adventure, if I can call it that. I came to Belgium with my international driver's license, so getting around was not supposed to be a hassle. I got a car immediately even though the one I ordered took about three months to arrive. While I waited for my order, the car dealership gave me a small car to drive.

Initially, finding my way around town was a bit daunting as I was not familiar with all the road markings. Driving was not a task I was comfortable with. I didn't understand some specific driving rules, for example, the right-hand rule. The right-hand rule implies that you have to give way to the vehicle coming from your right when no road sign indicates otherwise.

I used the international driver's license for a while, then had to change it to the European one. I thought it would be a walk in the park. I was, after all, a pretty decent driver, wasn't I? I couldn't be more wrong! It was much more difficult than I imagined.

Would you believe I took the driving test more than five times before I passed? I even lost count at some point. True story.

The test consisted of the theory aspect where I was assessed on the rules and regulations. I had to pass the theory before I could move on to the manoeuvres and road tests.

The computer-based test consisted of forty questions out of which three were considered serious questions. One was allowed to fail only one of these three questions. I missed two!

Why? The questions were in the official Belgian languages: French and Flemish, and I couldn't properly interpret the questions even though I had booked the mandatory licensed translator.

After the third attempt, I had to enrol in a driving school for theory classes as mandated by the law. It was difficult finding a school where classes were taught in English. I finally found one, but it was far from my neighbourhood. I had to travel a distance to get there. In addition, the school had classes in the evenings because the owner was only available from 1900 hours.

Because I had failed my test, I wasn't allowed to drive anymore. I had to rely on a driver to take me for lessons since my husband was often away for work and there was no public transport to my area after 1800 hours. I remember it being already dark and most times, cold, while I went for classes. It often felt like the day was already over.

Despite the darkness and the cold, I enjoyed the lessons. The instructors were nice and funny, and there were many other foreigners who were in the same shoes as me. I became friends with them, and we would often tease one another as people who couldn't pass the simple written driving test. It's safe to say we were comrades in failure. We also joked about the competence of the translators, who were sometimes more confusing than the actual questions.

After the lessons, I cleared the theories at one sitting. That day was special. I danced as David did in the Bible. If you saw me, you would think I had won the lottery. It was such a relief.

The manoeuvres and road tests were no issue for me either because I already had experience driving, but I did that twice. Twice because at the first attempt, I made a silly mistake on the road — I was meant to press a button in the car to clear the mist because the weather was foggy. But I didn't and the Belgian examiner wouldn't overlook it. The second time, however, I aced it and became a certified European driver. Finally!

The Bible says everything works together for our good. I believe that because I attended the driving school with the additional instructions, I know the traffic rules better than an average driver on the road, and that's a plus for me.

While there, we took many tours in Europe. Because Belgium is at the centre of Europe, it was easy to connect to other countries. We visited Luxembourg, one of the smallest countries on that continent; The Netherlands, to check out the red-light district; Germany, to have a taste of their sausages; France, to shop and to visit the Eiffel Tower; Portugal, where I enjoyed sardina for lunch always; and beautiful Spain, for their Spanish cuisines (paella).

God smiled on us again with a promotion to move to another European country. We left the summer of 2007 but kept our Belgium home till December of that year.

In Belgium, I cherished my yesterdays, I dreamt of my tomorrows, and I lived my todays. I discovered that a life without cause is a life without effect and that life is an experiment, the more experiments you make the better.

POSTCARD FROM THE EXPAT'S WIFE

Before the move, consider the language.

Will language be an issue? What support would your company provide? Would you need to enrol in a language school before the assignment or after you have landed? Find answers to these questions.

Moving into a country where you do not speak or understand the language can be tough, so be equipped with your pocket language dictionary, Google map and contact details of your local guide or friends.

Chapter Five

THE CITY OF SURPRISES

'Crossing a cultural border requires emotional and self-learning skills rather than simple intellectual and cognitive learning.'

~ McCall & Hollenbeck

We got news!

You know how it feels when your boss calls and says, 'By the way, I have something to discuss with you...' The discussion was about a promotion, and it came with another move. Romania was to become our new home.

Prior to that news, I had heard quite a bit about Romania from many sources, including the youth group of the church we attended. They had gone on a missionary trip to Romania and returned with lots of stories, most of which were not so good because they went to the interior suburbs to help poor people.

At the time, I thought Romania was not my cup of tea, so I didn't pay attention to their woebegone stories. I never had the faintest idea that our destinies were going to be connected to that country soon.

Well, as the saying goes, 'Never say never.' I should have known better.

When it became apparent that we would have to move to the eastern bloc, our opinions became divided. We had to choose between moving with the breadwinner of the family or staying back in Belgium to continue enjoying our waffles and chocolates.

We had become fond of Belgium and were well-grounded there. After seven years, it had become our home with a lot of memories. We had accepted the weather that we couldn't change, we loved the foods — Belgian chocolates, waffles, fries, and snails. In short, life was good or as we would say in Belgium, *la vie est belle.*

It was in Belgium that my husband was offered the choice of changing his nationality, an offer that he proudly declined. He's a proud and patriotic Nigerian.

When we got the news of the move, I told my husband he would have to move alone because I was scared of starting all over again after all I had been through. After many conversations for and against, we concluded that he would go ahead of us to resume his job while the children and I would stay back in Belgium. Thus, we officially started the split family phase where he would return home for the weekend and leave on Sunday evenings.

This back-and-forth phase went on for three months until the children started missing the presence of their father at home. The constant commuting was also taking its toll on my husband because he wasn't eating and resting well.

He worked late and always had to leave the office early on Fridays so as not to miss his flight back home. At home, he didn't often get enough rest because he would always leave again on Sunday evenings. The cost also was not friendly to the family purse.

We had to go back to the drawing board to agree on what was best for us. In life, most of the compromises we would have to make will be to support our family and to promote their best interest. For me, leaving behind the enjoyment and familiarity of Belgium and moving to Romania was one of those uneasy compromises. We eventually had to move, saying goodbye to the beautiful relationships we had built through the years and leaving the familiar for the unknown once again.

***

According to Romanian history, the decade-long rule of Nicolas Ceausescu became increasingly draconian through the 1980s until he was overthrown and executed in late 1989. In April 2005, Bucharest signed an EU accession treaty, paving the way for Romania to eventually join the union in January 2007. We moved to Bucharest in August of that year.

Romanians generally are good people with a family-oriented culture. They love foreigners, are kind, open-minded and always ready to grab any opportunity to learn something new. The older generation is religious with serious Orthodox Christian tendencies. Literacy in Romania is high and most Romanians living in the cities and towns can speak other languages like English, French and German. They are also very informed people in arts, sciences, and information technology. Still, they would stare at a black person and sometimes make inappropriate statements: an indication that some people still have a narrow view of the world.

I noticed the hard stares at marketplaces or even in supermarkets. I had expected that being in Europe, people would exhibit a bit of courtesy, but no! Some stared and others even uttered politically incorrect statements.

In Belgium, my children were in a school that was using the British curriculum. Being a Nigerian, with our school system tailored towards the British system, I automatically preferred the British one. We were informed that the A Level route was a better academic choice for students aspiring to further their education in the United Kingdom.

Before we moved to Romania, I began searching for a good British school for the children. I used the internet a lot, spoke to people and told the teachers in my children's school that we would be moving and were looking for a good British school for them. They gave their advice and suggested I look through the internet. At this time, there weren't many reputable international schools in Bucharest other than the American and British schools.

We saw a British International School, but it was small and hosted within an apartment. I knew it was best not to put our son in such a place. Dami was very energetic at that age and putting him in a place with such a small space would drive everybody in the school crazy. He needed a place to run around and engage in sports.

For my daughter, I might not have had an issue with the space but I didn't want her in one school and her brother in another. I discovered that the American school was the best option for my children, yet I continued to look for a British school. When I couldn't find any suitable one, I went back to the American school to check again.

There was nothing to not like about the American International School of Bucharest (AISB). As soon as my children stepped foot on the premises, they fell in love with it. I did, too — from the school meals to free computers for the children. I couldn't believe they would feed the children for free. We were paying for our children's meals in the British school in Belgium (BSB), but in AISB, they got to eat at no cost. A free meal was a big relief; topped with cheaper tuition, we were wowed.

What could be more fantastic?

The school excelled in academics and extracurricular activities. With qualitative education and well-structured academics, my children had it all. They learned new sports and engaged in many social events of which the rules of some were unfamiliar. They were happy and gradually forgot about all they missed from Belgium.

My children were super busy doing the right things children their ages should be doing, and I couldn't complain. AISB felt like home.

The AISB also gave me the chance to learn a thing or two about American culture and the academic system. Even though I had visited America many times, enjoying many trips as a tourist and having fun at incredible places like Disney World, I had never thought much about the American education system or its cultural nuances.

It was AISB that eventually gave me more than a window of knowledge about America. I have to state that anything I write here about the school is, of course, entirely my own opinion.

The Parents Teachers Association (PTA) was vibrant and fun. The social arm of the PTA organised relevant and enjoyable activities and events regularly. Parents had fun with what was available both within the school and outside in the city. We had opportunities to go out together to visit and shop for vegetables, home décor and small artefacts in the local markets. We also took turns carpooling.

The disco nights were phenomenal. We became young again as we danced to our favourite music or chatted about current affairs. The restaurants offered a wide range of food selections, from American to local. After each event, the ladies would always feel refreshed to take on the world again. The welcome barbeque at AISB was always great. Terry Fox Run too was fun-filled.

AISB was my favourite school, and I couldn't have asked for a better school community. I got a real chance to showcase Africa to the school community at the international day event. I met Stanley Nwobia, a Nigerian artist and writer in Bucharest who was invited to bring his books about Nigerian folktales and stories to the event. It was a big market for him as he sold almost all the copies he brought. The African community in town supported us massively.

A South African drum teacher from the British school also brought his African drums for display and gave free lessons on the spot to anyone interested. Many children enrolled in the private drum lessons. We played Fela's music to which many people danced. That day, many people became genuinely interested in the African music genre.

In addition, a student looking for an opportunity to make money took an African hair braiding stand. I encouraged her by supplying colourful beads and hairpieces. She made enough money for her whole tuition in one day. It was a blast!

One day, I received a phone call, 'Hello, Mrs. Oloidi. I am....' The person introduced herself and continued, 'We would like to invite you to attend a board interview to join the Education Policy Committee of the AISB.'

I was quite surprised because I hadn't applied for a job. It turned out that my husband's friend had nominated me. The interview was a questioning session to know whether I was suitable for the role. With my teaching qualifications, I easily passed and went ahead to serve as a member of the committee for two years.

Meetings were held once a month to discuss the school curriculum and other academic issues. I learned a lot from this experience, while offering quality contributions from previous experiences in the international schools we had attended before moving to Bucharest. It was an impactful service to the school and students.

I missed this community a lot when we finally had to leave for another assignment, but I made sure to tell the school authorities how much of a great job they were doing. I thanked them for the wonderful time we had with them.

The greatest secrets are often hidden in the most unlikely places. AISB in Bucharest was one of those secrets for us, considering how hard we fought not to come to Romania.

***

The cultures we encountered included not only the host countries' cultures, but also those of the international community — the cultures of other expatriates from their different home countries, the culture of the organisation we worked for, and others. Each culture and subculture had its own set of morals and assumptions.

Greengate Estate was my family's first experience of living in a compound with many houses and it was impressive. It was a good place to live and raise children. The Greengate compound played many roles for my family. It was a home, a safe nest, a community, and a learning hub. The residents looked out for one another's interests. Neighbours played and learned together.

There were twenty-five houses and almost all of them were occupied by expats. Our children blended and bonded with ease as majority of them attended the same school.

In this warm community, I enjoyed Rekah's Indian cuisines and they enjoyed my jollof rice and turkey menu. Paula, an Italian lady was my Italian menu teacher; she made the best Italian pasta sauces and *to-die-for* tiramisu; I have never tasted anything like it elsewhere.

I tried so many other delicacies because I love food and I wasn't shy about it. I also love to cook, so we exchanged a lot of recipes. I was fond of Thai curry and Indian *chapati*, enjoyed *raclette* and binged on *samale*.

I had the best time of my life organising and

inviting friends for dinners. Romania brought the best out of me!

It was not customary to move to a new country and have friends waiting for me, but Romania gave me that opportunity. I call it grace. Before I moved to Romania, a friend from the International Women Association (IWA) had linked me up with another friend, Laila. Laila took care of me and showed me many places. She introduced me to the women's club where I met other ladies like Natalia who had lived in Nigeria before she moved to Romania. We connected immediately and remain friends until today.

We were a group of ladies without paid employment even though we worked in different capacities. What could we possibly do when our children were in school and we had free time available? We either went for lunch or simply met for coffee.

After a while, it became monotonous, so each of us started offering ideas to make good use of our spare time. Out of the many suggestions made, studying the Bible was top on the list since many of us were Christians.

We started the Baneasa bible study group, which I led for over two years. Together, we studied many books by Christian female authors like Beth Moore, Paula White, Sheila Walsh and Anne Graham, to mention just a few. We shared love and food and supported one another in prayers.

We encouraged each other to remain in the love of God and introduced other people to the group. We became grounded in God's word — the highlight of my Romania experience.

The church has always been an important part of my family focus. In Romania, the International Baptist Church (IBC) in Bucharest was our home church. We always went to international churches because they catered to a medley of people and different denominations and were mostly meant for non-locals. An international church was often home to Christians from India, Mexico, America, England, Germany, and other nations who had either migrated for work or who lived there for one reason or the other.

Church was where we spoke the same language. Outside the church, if you told somebody, 'I will be praying for you' for instance, some of them would look at you like you were crazy. Someone once asked me, 'Did I tell you I believe in God?' when I told them 'God bless you.' The thing is that I am used to saying, 'God bless you' but on this occasion, the recipient didn't have the same belief I did, so I had to apologise. In church, I could tell someone, 'God bless you' or 'Merry Christmas' and they would receive it with joy.

Church allowed us to be ourselves and to take on leadership roles like hosting Bible study, leading women's meetings, prayer meetings and teaching in Sunday school. S.O. served as an elder while I served as a deaconess. It appeared that we always got a chance to serve in God's house wherever we went.

We hosted many Bible studies together with church members in our home, serving with gladness. Our children grew to love God. Every year, there was a summer barbeque for the church family and an annual retreat in Brasov. It was always a great time to get to know each other as a family of Christ.

Church also allowed us to mingle with different people from different backgrounds that we could never have met otherwise. For some of them, it was also their first time speaking to black people. Nobody made anyone feel less of themselves in the IBC. It was not a citadel of perfection, but we quickly settled misunderstandings and moved on.

The pastor and his wife Naty were not just spiritual leaders for us but friends also. Naty has inspired me in many ways. As a pastor's wife, she held her position with poise, diligence and grace as to the Lord. As a friend, she helped me many times to see things from the right perspectives and she has been a great encouragement even in writing this book.

Many events got me expectant, the IBC women's conference is one of them. During the event, many women from around the world would converge in a hotel in a selected country for the weekend. It was always a delightful gathering.

The atmosphere was always spiritually charged with experienced Christian women speakers. The activities were always impactful and garnished with practical lessons. The IBC women always made the conferences a wholesome experience for me. Serving God is never boring.

I had the opportunity to plan the Bulgarian version with my friend Naty. It brought glory to God and was a blessing to many, particularly me.

***

I have come to discover that what we anticipate seldom occurs and what we least expect generally happens. My husband hates surprises even today. Surprising him always ended up taking a different turn as he would always end up surprising me instead. It is often as if he has a third ear and a third eye. Nevertheless, on this occasion, I wanted to appreciate him and I surely beat him to it. I perfected my plans so that he didn't suspect that our guests were there for his birthday because I always had friends over for either lunch or dinner.

I had my guests list ready, sent out the invites, arranged for the caterer and got everything set up for the beautiful day. My friends helped me a lot in the planning. They helped with setting up my garden and decorating it without him knowing about it.

I made the party arrangements with a friend of his who took him out early for us to get the house and the garden set up. The caterer arrived with food and our guests started trooping in. My husband arrived at his party unaware and unprepared. It was a good way of saying thank you for all he had been doing. It was a wonderful party and we all had fun.

***

It's no secret that Romania felt like home to us. We loved it and decided to immerse ourselves in its culture. I did a bit of language study, but my children picked most of their vocabulary from school and the street.

We loved the sound of the Latin-derived language. We all knew our *mulțumesc* (thank you), *la mulți ani (happy birthday or happy new year), bună dimineața* (good morning), and *bună seara (good evening)*.

And the food? We enjoyed the local dishes: *mămăligă* cu *brânza* (polenta with cream cheese), *mici* (the local minced meat known as suya in Nigeria), and *sarmale* (cabbage stuffed with rice).

Romania has many interesting cities and towns — Cluj-Napoca, Brasov, Timișoara, Ploiesti, Oradea, Constanta and so on. I paid my dues, saw and conquered the country, and I loved every bit of it. It was a beautiful sight and there was no blood-sucking vampire in Dracula's castle.

I had pizza at the popular *Pizza la Maria* în Timișoara, danced in the club in Cluj, took the Transfagarasan Road even though I wouldn't recommend it for a faint-hearted person.

While in Romania, we visited many other countries on holidays, including Bulgaria, Cyprus, United States, Canada and Turkey. Our ultimate holiday experience was in Antalya in Turkey. It's a tourist destination for everybody who wants a relaxing getaway. In Antalya, everyone minded their business. I think the city was designed for tourists, so one could walk around in their bikini and shorts and nobody would care. Everyone went there to enjoy themselves.

There were so many hotels, fully equipped with everything you needed such that you didn't have to leave the hotel to enjoy the luxury of the place. If you wanted to swim, you would find swimming pools and a beach right in the hotel. If you wanted to party every night, there was a party outlet. For those who loved to club, they didn't need to leave the hotel to have a clubbing experience. If all you wanted to do was eat all day, there was food. Wherever you turned, station by station, you would find food there. My children would go to get food at 0300 hours and go swimming at the beach around 0100 hours. Till date, the holiday in Antalya reverberates with them.

Speaking of my children, my son turned eighteen in Romania while still in high school. This was due to the constant changes in school as a result of our frequent moves. Although he left for college before he turned nineteen, the time before he left was a hassle. The Romanian government takes seriously the fact that adulthood begins at eighteen. We received an email from the government advising us that at that age, our son must leave home, be an adult, take responsibility and become accountable for his actions.

The knowledge that I was to send my son packing before he was ready was a rude shock for me. Totally unexpected.

Nonetheless, we had a good laugh about the notice and acted immediately. Since he was still in high school, we couldn't possibly send him away, so we supplied a letter from his school as proof that he was still in full academic study.

We were told that he must have had community service hours and if he was to continue residing on our property, he must pay rent to us. We swiftly got him enrolled with an NGO for his community hours and handled all paperwork for him to be able to stay in our house for that summer before he proceeded to university.

Hodding Carter was right when he said '... there are only two lasting bequests we can hope to give our children. One of these is roots, the other, wings.' That period was eye opening. We had a good discussion about being an adult and taking responsibility. It was also a good chance to prepare our daughter for what was ahead.

Many of our friends also had similar experiences with their children. One of them went as far as buying a suitcase for his son. The suitcase served as a symbol, letting the young man know that he was just a tenant in their home and if he did not behave himself or abide by the rules and regulations, he could be sent packing.

That is European life. Nobody lives off the other, everyone must earn their livelihood.

Was it all rosy in Romania? Of course not. Even though I do not intend to fill my story with all the sad moments or events, some experiences need to be shared to bring balance. There were moments when people would look at me as if I was an apparition or a criminal.

I stopped going to an orphanage in town because many people would stare harshly at me. Even the children would cry nonstop at me because they were not used to seeing people with my skin colour, at least that was the only explanation I had for the incessant wails that would erupt whenever I approached them.

These experiences do something to one's self-confidence. When you go to the market and somebody thinks that because you're black, they can harass you; or when you enter a shop and people look at you like you're a criminal or less than human, you may begin to wonder what you are. I think people who do that are people who have been living in their cocoon — people who have never left their immediate environment before — and it is pitiful.

There were people who asked me what type of food we eat in Africa and seemed to think that it was probably the food that made us dark in complexion. In response, I would either invite them over or we would organise a potluck where everybody brought food from their country.

We had a friend whose husband was an ambassador. They were transferred to Nigeria and when they were leaving, she hosted us and served Mexican food, which I enjoyed. Then another friend organized a send-forth party to honour our friends and asked everyone to bring food from their country. I made fried rice and beef. In about five minutes, the fried rice was gone.

A lady congratulated me as if I had done something unimaginable. Bewildered, I asked, 'Why are you congratulating me? Did you think people wouldn't like my food or that I don't know how to cook?' I have no idea what she was thinking. Those were some of the subtle biases we encountered.

Some were not so subtle. I remember this cleaner who worked in a house close to ours. Each morning, she would arrive when I was taking my children to join the school bus. I noticed that each day she saw me, she would make a sign of the cross.

One morning I pointed at her—since she did not speak English—and said, 'You make the sign of the cross. I wonder what it is you see in me that makes you make the sign of the cross. I see it in you too. I am also making the cross sign.' Then I crossed myself too. Quite dramatic of me, right? Oh, but the expression on her face afterwards! It was satisfying. Afterwards, I spoke with her employer about the incident and spared her no other thought.

Those were moments that were not so pleasant. Other than that, we had a lot of good memories in Romania — memories worth reminiscing about.

All too soon, as it was meant to happen, it was time for us to pack up and move again, and move we did. This time, to the land of beautiful mountains, designer watches, cheese, and milky chocolate.

POSTCARD FROM THE EXPAT'S WIFE

Upon arrival in the host location, don't lock yourself away. Take the opportunity and time to reinvent yourself.

It is possible that you would have more time on your hands than you would know what to do with. Do not wait for the weeks, months and years to roll by, just get busy.

Whatever you do, don't lose your sense of identity.

Chapter Six

REBELS BEWARE!

Living in a foreign culture is like playing a game you have never played before and for which the rules have not been explained very well. The challenge is to enjoy the game without missing too many plays, learning the rules and developing skills as you go along.

~R. Kohls

Switzerland is a beautiful, cool and clean country. I went in with very high expectations as I had heard only wonderful things about the country. At one point, I wondered if only angels lived there because the Swiss are very prim and proper.

It is a general belief that an average Swiss person is not funny and lacks a sense of humour. That is not necessarily true. They have been known to make jokes at their own expense. Here are some popular jokes that even a Swiss would laugh at.

'You know a Swiss when they:
Spit out Belgian chocolate in disgust.
Make reservations to see a movie.

Are surprised when you're not delayed by road works.
Think spontaneity is OK, but only if it's planned.
Make an appointment to do their own laundry in their own apartment building.'[4]

I laughed really hard when I read this joke. Having lived in Switzerland for four years, I can easily relate.

Initially, when we moved, I was not sure what life would be like living in Switzerland. It was said that it is impossible to criticize the country other than for the fact that it is a very expensive European country to live in. I was not disappointed and even though some things weren't as expected, they were not terrible.

I got my fair share of fines because I could not stay out of traffic offences, and I found myself getting speeding or parking tickets. Most times, it was not intentional; Switzerland had a lot of parking offences.

The moment you move into a community in Switzerland, you are expected to register yourself at the local office, so they know where you live. Then they would give you a disc and a printed copy of their many rules and regulations.

[4]culled from www.thelocal.ch

The disc was used to determine how long a vehicle had been parked on a particular parking space. You were to put the disc in your car in a manner that allowed the checker to see the time displayed the moment you parked your vehicle. Sometimes, I would forget to display the disc on my dashboard, thereby preventing the checker from being able to determine how long my car had been parked there. This would automatically attract a fine.

Those are the kinds of rules I broke because most of the time, I just needed to dash in to pick up an item, but I would get there and find the cashier line to be so long or I would get carried away by window shopping. Before you could say *jack*, thirty minutes would have gone by and if I was unlucky, the checker would pick the number and the fine would arrive in my letterbox.

I also faulted on speed limits. Oftentimes, I would have a meeting for 0900 hours at a distant location, but I would not leave home early enough. In my haste, I would exceed the speed limits and end up getting caught by the cameras. Whenever this happened, I usually would not say a word about it to my husband. Then when the fine arrived, my husband would be surprised that I had driven through that route. Oops!

With the Swiss, communication is explicit and direct; sincerity and clarity are respected. The Swiss are generally self-confident, not loud or exuberant, but are very great listeners.

I discovered this and a lot more from my landlord. He wanted to get to know the people living in his house and because I was curious too, it was like a balanced equation. I asked many questions and he was happy to answer them. By this act, he was also able to understand a bit of where I was coming from.

I discovered so much about the average Swiss person through my neighbours as well. While I cannot say we had a thriving relationship, we did hang out occasionally. I got invited to small garden parties and in the summer, they let me enjoy fruits from their gardens. Some of them would bring flower bouquets to my door, so I could share in the spring fragrances.

From the little interaction I had with them, I can say a little about an average Swiss person. I discovered that they are cautious toward new people and would always want to start off on the right foot. They appreciate politeness and sincerity, and thoroughly abide by the rules. For instance, if the law says one cannot wash their car or mow the lawn at a particular time, the Swiss will adhere strictly to it. They are also formal. I was never referred to by my first name, only by my last name. Madam and *vous*[5] were terms they used to address me.

Swiss children are brought up to respect elders, to be hardworking and to be reliable. I found the Swiss people easy to deal with since it was easy to predict how a Swiss would behave in certain situations. Meetings are always by appointment, even for random coffee dates, and ladies dressed in formal wear.

Another important thing I noticed about the Swiss women is that family and family matters are precious to them. They are not keen on how much you would pay them; when it is time to close for business and go home to be with family, they would leave. No one could buy their time.

Je parle un peu français means 'I speak a little French'. I needed to sharpen my French language skill if I was to find it easy living in Geneva, Switzerland. So, the first thing I did was to enrol with a private teacher; she taught me in my home twice a week. Having a private tutor was one of the

[5]Vous is the formal way of addressing an individual in French

luxuries that came with my husband's job.

One thing I quickly learned, was that learning to speak a language is great only when you have opportunities to practice what you are learning. Sitting in a class or in front of a teacher or television would not help as much as having a physical interactive conversation with real people. This, unfortunately, was a luxury I did not enjoy. Everyone was busy and had no time for small talk. Alimesh my tutor was great and friendly, but she relocated to another country in the middle of my program. Soon, another tutor replaced her.

The new lady had had little or no contact with my kind before. It was difficult initially as she didn't know what to expect from an African English-speaking woman. After a bit of back and forth, we got to like and respect each other. We learnt a few things from each other and even had fun doing that. However, I changed from having the lesson twice to once a week while I looked for other opportunities to be out more and meet new people with whom to practice.

Boredom was not an option, especially because there is more to life than staying at home and learning a language that I was not using. I eventually stopped the lesson for something else.

My daughter's school resumed, and I was invited to the first PTA meeting in International School of Geneva, La Grande Boissière. The meeting was short and precise. During the meeting, I tried to connect with some ladies on a casual note and in the process, I saw a Belgian lady that I knew from our first assignment in Uzbekistan. She did not recognize me, but I am not one to ever forget people's faces, whether I meet them casually or formally. Her husband and mine worked for the same company.

I was happy to see a familiar face. Even when she did not recognize me at first glance, I called her name and introduced myself to jog her memory and we hugged cheerfully. She introduced me to some of the ladies as a new parent.

After the meeting, while going back home, I remember sitting next to a woman on the tram. I noticed she had been in the meeting too and we both exchanged pleasantries. Once we discovered that our children were in the same grade at school, we got chatty, discussing a few things about the school. I found out that she had been around for a while and knew her way around the school authorities and the building. I saw an opportunity for friendship.

'Where is home?' she asked.

This is a question I was asked more times than I was asked my name. People were often curious to know where we are from. After telling them we are Africans and not Americans, they either became disappointed or quickly believed that we must be diplomats. A misconception that revealed the world's biases against black people.

Africans are not thought of as expatriates, but as either economic immigrants or refugees. This was exactly why a man who came to do some repair work in my house asked me, 'Is your husband a white man?' That was the first question he thought to ask me. My family pictures were all over the house staring at him, yet his bias got the best of him. I used the opportunity to open his eyes to his prejudice.

Stella, my new friend, was not biased; she was just curious, so I quickly answered her question.

I replied, 'Heaven is home.'

Her eyes lit up at once. She gave me a genuine smile and a warm embrace.

'You must be a Christian then,' she declared.

My yes was a satisfying answer, and a new friendship was born. I was excited — my first friend in Geneva is a born again child of God. Wow! God is good. We exchanged phone numbers and hit it off from there. Goodbye to being new to town and welcome to a great sisters' fellowship.

From Bible study to prayer meetings to hanging out, from visiting shops to doing crafts, and from crafts to neighbourhood meetings. I love people, I love friendship, I love life and yes, I enjoy being sociable.

I joined the PTA and was sponsored for an executive position. My friend had held the position for a while, and she needed relief as she wanted to do something else with her life. Election Day came and I got the position.

I accepted to serve as a PTA representative, which was a volunteer position for the International Baccalaureate Creativity Action Service (IB CAS) Program.

CAS is one of the programs required for the fulfilment of the IB diploma. The CAS program is designed such that there are no rewards but there are consequences. Without completing each area, the students do not get awarded the IB diploma in their senior year.

I was told that it was a tough job that no one was willing to take. Truth be told, working with young adults is not always fun, especially concerning academic fulfilment. I was sceptical and reluctant because I was new and had little experience in this area. I asked a lot of questions and was introduced to the school staff whom I would be working with to facilitate the program. We met, exchanged ideas, and drew a plan.

We launched into action but as time went on, I discovered that I was alone on this journey as my companion was very busy with a lot of other school commitments. To wait for her or expect a lot from her would hamper my productivity, so I worked with my schedule and invited a few other parents to help with areas I was not very good at.

To rely on others for assistance was a tall order. After a while, I understood that everyone in Geneva was busy. No one came to Switzerland to slack; it was a very expensive city hence everyone was involved in doing one thing or the other for survival. There would be no assistance and I was on my own, which was good in a way because it allowed me work at my pace and make my own decisions.

We had the first phase, a bake sale, which was a sort of training ground for me. I got to understand the students and staff and got familiar with names. Later, we organized the *keremesse*, a Christmas flea market, in conjunction with the local community. It was a measure of my achievement regarding my experiences and working with the senior students. It was a huge success.

Through working with the IB class of 2014, I discovered that words only take meaning when acted on. While I worked with the students, I never asked them to do what I would not do with them. I gave only measurable tasks and monitored and engaged them throughout the process. We discussed ideas together and I gave them choices with boundaries. It was democratic but I remained in charge.

I also learned valuable lessons from my interactions with the senior year students. I learned that children are the same everywhere in the world. They learn to make good decisions by being part of the decision-making process rather than by just following directions. To get their attention, you have to speak their language and be like them. You must respect them and give clear guidance and instructions.

I had a good rapport and working relationship with all the students. We worked together as companions and had so much fun. I tried to see things from their perspective and cajoled them sometimes. We understood each other and I had their backs when necessary. They played their parts well and we had the best results that year.

I got a lot of accolades and felt appreciated, but I had to step down after my daughter graduated. Although I was asked to continue, I had no justification to do so since I was no longer a parent in the school and should no longer be in the PTA.

***

My experience in Belgium taught me that living abroad without a strong support base of friends and family could lead to serious health challenges. In Switzerland, I had my very strong and supportive husband and children.

Despite my husband's busy schedule, he would always check in with me to make sure I was fine. He made sacrifices to rekindle our love and to let me know that he appreciated me for everything. My husband and daughter did their best to make me feel loved and cared for, I never lacked anything, and I enjoyed their full support.

During my daughter's senior years in high school, sometimes during lunch break, she would call to ask if I wanted to join her for lunch. I would drive down to her school and we would have lunch together in the school cafeteria or somewhere else.

When she finally left for university, I began to feel lonely again. I was scared and afraid and I would sometimes cry. Thankfully, my husband stepped in. He reassured me of his care and would always call to ask where I was, what I was doing for lunch, and if I wanted to come to his office to have lunch with him.

On most days, I would walk with him to the office. It was a short distance from where we lived, about a thirty-minute walk. We would walk to the office together, then I would take the tram back home, or I could walk back. I walked back most of the time and the physical exercise helped me tremendously.

We would do the same after close of work. Sometimes, I would take the car to pick him. We did a lot together as he was travelling less at that point. He made sure to cover for my daughter's absence.

Additionally, I was beginning to meet more people and make more friends. Even though they were busy, we would sometimes agree to meet for lunch. A lot of my new friends worked with the United Nations so they would ask me to come to town for lunch, which I always gladly accepted.

Sometimes, I deceived myself by comparing the two worlds I had — life as a Nigerian and a European. As a Nigerian, I enjoy my vibrant culture, busy and activity-focused life, engaging in a lot of gatherings here and there, having friends and family surround us and celebrating holidays with a lot of friends and relatives. Whereas my life in Europe was active and satisfactory, but sometimes different from what I was used to. I tried to enjoy both worlds.

With age setting in and all that comes with it —

menopause and the attending hot flashes, sleeplessness, having to deal with adult children in a faraway country and the empty nest phase, it appeared too many things were happening at the same time. I decided to grab the bull by the horn and not wallow in self-pity. There had been many other times in my life that I had experienced being in a new environment: from high school to college, getting into a new job and even becoming a stay-at-home mum. If I managed to survive those times, I knew I would be fine this time too.

Over the years, I have learned to pray for things that would make my life richer, more fulfilled, and more blessed wherever I find myself. I learned to persist in prayer. Looking back now, it comforts my heart to say God is good. It was not always easy, but He has always been faithful.

Geneva is an expensive place to live in. It is an international city, very cosmopolitan and well structured. Hence, everyone seemed too busy to have the kind of close-knit activities I enjoyed in previous places. I plugged myself into many things, some out of pure interest while others were simply to keep myself busy like everyone else.

My schedule was filled with activities that included

walking in the botanical garden, sightseeing, neighbourhood trailing to discover new and interesting little havens in and around town, Bible studies, prayer meetings and language lessons. I did quite a bit to blend in and to get busy in Geneva, Switzerland.

Once in a while, I served at the famous soup kitchen. I was also a registered volunteer with the Serve the City Organisation (www.servethecitygeneva.ch) in Geneva, collecting food and other household items for later distribution to the less privileged. I sat on the board of Sesor, an NGO founded by another Nigerian and a sister in Christ.

Finally, an opportunity came to do something worthwhile. I enrolled in an off-campus program for a diploma degree in ministry. It was a two-year program, mostly online.

We got study materials online and bought some hardcopy books. I connected with other students, interacted with my professors, and did everything online except for the classroom experience every six weeks. It was a very tedious ordeal to sit from 0900 hours to 1800 hours. The first few experiences were killing for me as an adult. Sitting for long is not my thing; my attention span was short, and I just hated it. But as time went by, I got better at sitting and paying more attention. It took a while for me to adjust to learning the coursework and meeting assignment deadlines, but I got everything done in record time.

My supervisor was a beautiful lady from Uganda, accomplished, helpful and a great listener. I gained a lot from her experiences and supervision, her attention to detail and her never taking half measures towards work. All of these helped shape me to gain new perspectives in life.

Some of the other students became my friends; we evaluated and validated one another, prayed together and shared experiences, exchanged ideas about one another's research work and helped one another to become better.

The programme provided another great outlet for me to interact with others. I had enough schoolwork to keep me busy, I had myself to look after in the area of keeping fit and pampering myself, and I had my project to plan and execute. All these things got me busy, and I could not be happier.

The study offered me a great opportunity to think

wide with real support from other students, but it was difficult to choose a topic for research. I prayed as if everything depended on it, sought counsel, asked questions, collaborated with other people and as a result, 'The Master Key' was adopted. As soon as my supervisor and the professor in charge approved the topic, I swung into action.

I got books, read journals and spoke with people to get the ball rolling. I had launched the Master Key earlier as a personal project to bring women together to start praying for our church, our communities and our family needs. I looked for other women to join in the vision, my church family keyed into it and we started with six women in March 2014.

We led the Crossroad Prayer Ministry to support the existing church prayer group. We recorded many answered prayers plus many new members and God was lifted. I decided to make this my official project since it has the same mission of touching lives and helping others. It was accepted and adopted as one of the requirements for the fulfilment of my diploma program. The Master Key prayer group is still alive today.

After fulfilling that desire of getting a diploma, it

was time to start something else to keep myself busy and sane. I started playing with the idea of writing a book.

To bring this to reality, I attended the prestigious Annual Writers' Conference in Switzerland. The conference had in attendance experts and professionals. I must say I became intimidated, sitting in the same room with several award-winning authors and uniquely gifted writers.

I thought to myself, *I am not a writer. I couldn't possibly measure up.* But I decided to at least try to pen down my experiences. That was when the idea of this book was birthed. I knew I had to tell my story as an African trailing spouse. The story of an African moving to Europe, living among Europeans, imbibing the host culture and yoking together, bringing about a blend of the two worlds. Sometimes, enjoying the European life and at other times, claiming my *Africanness* to a fault.

Soon, it was time again to pick my bags and move as usual. This time, to the Arab world. We began with the preparations as moving is always daunting: from moving personal belongings to ensuring the house is in perfect condition for the owner, settling all bills and making sure to cancel out all registrations, selling cars, taking care of finances, and all the other necessary but exhausting tasks.

Our house exit inspection was more difficult than the entry, but everything went well. The agent was impressed and thankful that the house was in excellent condition even after we had lived in it for four years.

When my family was to move into the house, she did not know what to expect from a black family. We saw the house and my daughter had instantly fallen in love with it, insisting that whatever it took, she wanted to live in it — a beautiful neighbourhood, a lovely and airy building, a modern Swiss home — we all fell in love with it. Leaving the house in the same condition it was when we leased it four years ago, the agent could not help but thank me profusely.

Goodbye was painful to say. I found myself getting teary and all choked up by the simple word, goodbye. Nevertheless, I garnered the courage to say, 'Goodbye, Switzerland. Goodbye to my beautiful city, Geneva and goodbye to Europe.'

Those sixteen good years in Europe were wonderful beyond doubt. I saw the world through the eyes of the Swiss, and I could boldly say there is one God, one world and one humanity. I remain thankful for the wonderful people that I met, the many acquaintances and the good friends. I am extremely thankful to God for the Switzerland experience.

POSTCARD FROM THE EXPAT'S WIFE

Upon arrival in the host location, motivate yourself!

It may not necessarily be an intellectually stimulating environment, but you must try to make yourself productive. If the environment is right and conducive for your family, get more degrees or learn something new.

Chapter Seven

FUN TIME!

Culture is an integrated system of learned behaviour patterns that are characteristic of members of a society. It is a total way of life of a particular group of people—everything that the group thinks, says, does and makes.

~M. Pusch

Think Dubai, Think holiday, right?

Dubai never fails to impress me. I have seen it a couple of times yet with every visit, I am always wowed by its beauty and greatness. The UAE boasts of many interesting things amongst which are its rich culture, Burj Al Arab (considered by many to be the only seven-star hotel in the world), and Burj Khalifa (the tallest building in the world). Dubai is a dynamic city teeming with expats.

Probably everyone living today wants to see this desert that has turned into a 21st Century wonder. In Dubai, English and Arabic are widely spoken.

One would easily feel at home there without ever having a boring time.

The news of our relocation to Dubai came when I least expected it. I was getting used to Switzerland and Geneva was gradually becoming home. I had found my band of women and life was going fine, so why would I think of relocating?

Once again, I dragged my feet about this new development but soon made up my mind to get on with it. We started making plans and moved in June 2016, but we did not arrive in Dubai until August.

We took the time to do other things; we visited the United Kingdom and stopped to see our children in Canada. As our daughter was turning twenty, we spent time with her to make her celebration memorable. It was after we had spent quality time with them that we started our adventure, or what you may call a second honeymoon in Dubai.

We arrived at the Dubai International Airport after about twelve hours of flight. I was tired and jet-lagged but the vibrancy right from the airport energized and reinvigorated my spirit. The number of people at the airport was overwhelming but in no time, we passed through immigration and customs, ready for a new life in a completely different world.

I cannot say that I remember to thank God all the time but this one time, I recall looking at myself and reminiscing on my story. With the way my life had been, I could not but burst into songs of praise and thanksgiving. I sang, prayed, and praised. I felt the grace of God and his goodness to me and my family. All I could do was show gratitude. I was reminded of the word of prophet in Isaiah 25:1 (New International Version):

> *'Lord you are my God, I will exalt and praise your name, for in perfect faithfulness you have done wonderful things, things planned long ago.'*

We arrived at the hotel where we were again greeted by the usual Arabian hospitality. We were led to our suite and beautiful is an understatement. There is nothing small about Dubai; everything is big, cheerful, and beautiful. I cannot begin to describe the interiors of our hotel suite; it was more than impressive.

I quickly settled in and rearranged the room to suit

my purpose. We had made some arrangements with the hotel manager; it was to be our home for more than a month. However, a building construction going on beside the hotel caused us so much unease and when we could not tolerate it any longer, we terminated the agreement and moved to a better hotel nearby.

The new hotel was also beautiful with the added benefit of being in the marina area with a view of the sea. The rooms were spacious with conveniences. I could either do my cooking or eat out because of the hotel's proximity to many restaurants. From my window, I could enjoy the beautiful sea and the beach. There was also a cinema next door. With a VIP ticket at the cinema, you got your snacks delivered to you and a personal orderly to help you with your blankets. You could even lay to watch your movies as if you were in your sitting room. Pure pleasure!

I felt I was living in luxury, something inessential but conducive for comfort and pleasure. Dubai has a way of spoiling someone if money is not a problem. It is easy to forget who you are and just soak in the pleasure and comfort the United Arab Emirates has to offer.

The hotel's breakfast was out of this world. We enjoyed different cuisines from continental to British to regional. I did not miss any breakfast. My husband, on the other hand, was not a breakfast person but I still ensured that he ate something before he left for work.

Having lived in Europe, which is known for its supply of great wine, I occasionally indulge in a glass or two. However, alcoholic beverages are not readily available to everyone in Dubai, so we needed to find how we could get a reasonable supply. After much ado, we got to understand the way it worked. In no time, we got the necessary permit and were able to get a bottle or two. I will not write extensively about this, but I am willing to give personal tips about this to anyone desiring to know.

I experienced a bit of a culture shock in Dubai, things that would get the feminist agitators dumbfounded. Men could get away with some things that their female counterparts would be reprimanded for. For example, modesty in dressing is essential for the women but the men are allowed to wear their shorts and t-shirts. There were many instances that made me wonder what was going on but was told that was their culture. I had to mind my own business. Many times, S.O. would remind me to be careful as Dubai was not Europe. I had to warn my female guests visiting that they could only dress in certain ways and were not allowed to behave in certain manners. This is Dubai where your rights stop at the airport. I accepted it and we had fun anyway.

On a deeper reflection, it allowed me to appreciate life and other cultures. This is one of the reasons travelling is viewed as learning — a journey to see through the history and cultures of other people, to appreciate diversity and differences.

***

It took us forever to start the process of getting a house. In the UAE, you needed your permits and documentations in order to rent a house and the process took longer than usual for us.

For some reasons, I got sick of the hotel life and needed to start my life in Dubai. I wanted to do things that would help me get back into my usual routine; I was tired of living out of suitcases. I knew nobody there and social media was controlled. I had gotten tired of the nonstop shopping and started getting cranky yet again. God answered my prayers.

Our documentations were sorted, and we began searching for a house; a process that was harder than I had thought it would be. There were many beautiful houses but there was usually one issue or the other. There was one apartment I saw that had everything I wanted in a house but then a telephone mast was right next to it, and I could not take the risk. My health is very important to me.

I remembered that in Belgium there was an outcry when a huge mast was going to be erected next to the international school. Upon research, I discovered that it is dangerous to have a mast next to a residential building. I declined to take the house beside the mast with a feeling of sadness.

House-hunting was stressful; it was either the house was too big, or not close enough to what we needed, or the conditions that came with renting was cumbersome.

It seemed we were a bit unlucky with getting a good house at that time of the year. However, not too long after, our patience paid off and we got a beautiful Arabian-style house with a lovely drive-through, a garage for two cars, a sizable swimming pool and a manageable garden.

The property itself needed a little touch-up, but we took it because I wanted it. I got the owner to sign an undertaking that he would do the necessary adjustments within a month. We moved in but it took forever for him to honour the agreement. I had to threaten a lawsuit to which he did not budge. That was when I found out that he was not the real owner, he was just a front for the owner.

I snooped around before I eventually got the owner's phone number. We spoke and finally, the miracle happened. The house was done and we were happy to live in it.

***

'Mabrook', my examiner said.

'What does that mean?' I asked.

'Mabrook. Do you know what it means?' he repeated as if he had not heard my question.

'I have an idea', I replied.

'Okay?'

'It means congratulations,'

'Yes. I'm pleased to tell you that you've passed.'

I needed to hear those words to have my freedom. Living on Jumeirah Islands without being able to drive was not funny. Relying on taxis and friends to pick me up was not easy for me either. In Dubai, your driver's license is dependent on your passport. If your passport was from one of the countries whose driver's licenses were not accepted or approved in the UAE, you would have to register in a driving school to obtain a license.

I had heard so much about driving tests in Dubai, and I was weary. Having driven in Europe for fifteen years I had a record of being a very careful and great driver. But in Dubai, it did not matter how many years of driving experience you had as long as you held a passport from one of 'those' countries. It was possible for one to choose either the fast track or the normal process. I chose the fast track.

The driving license journey was threefold: First, the theory which I passed at once; then the manoeuvres, I also did this without hassles; and the final stage, which was the actual road test. All of these could take three months or more.

My instructor was a pleasant lady from India, so pleasant that we formed a friendship. Because we became friends, she did more for me than an average instructor, giving me tips and staying extra time with me to practice.

The evening before my test she asked, 'Do you mind if we have a special final practice?'

'No,' I replied, delighted that she would go out of her way to do so for me.

Unfortunately, something came up and she could not be with me. However, she arranged with her friend to help. Another friendship started. We did what we needed to do, and she reassured me of how good I was and that I could do it.

The next day, I woke up early and was ready for my test. I was the first to arrive at the centre, except for the examiner who was there before all of us. He called me first and two others. We went off to the road and I was the first to drive. It should not have been a problem, but I was accustomed to a shift gear car whereas I was given an automatic car to drive.

On this very day, I did my best not to make my struggle obvious, but the examiner still noticed. She asked if I had been driving before to which I said yes. I became unsure after that question but still did my thing.

One of the ladies that was with me in the driving test told me it was her fifth time. 'You will pass this time. Since you are coming with me, it's going to be your lucky day.' I assured her.

And it was. Every one of us passed.

I became free to run my errands and control my time. I started making efforts to be involved in more activities now that I could go about without any hassles. I joined a women's group and resumed my usual routine.

I should not bore you with my unending stories of church activities, but I believe it is worth mentioning that Dubai is truly cosmopolitan where you can find everything, including churches.

Fellowship of the Emirates is a big church in Dubai with three services every Friday. Always, we preferred the early morning worship service from 0700 hours to 0900 hours or the second service from 1000 hours to noon.

I met other ladies. We studied the word, made friends, prayed together and encouraged one another. We celebrated every achievement and reckoned with our differences as it was a collection of women from around the world and different Christian backgrounds. It was my community of ladies.

***

If you are fortunate enough, you will find someone who brightens your day and inspires you, someone who will always give you an ear regardless of the time, space or situation.

I grew up in a family where friendship matters a lot. Both my parents were hospitable, and my mum was incredible. I grew up knowing some of her friends as family members only to be told later that they were not blood relations but friends.

I too have been blessed with some great friends in this lifetime. I have also been told a couple of times that I am hospitable. I guess I got it from my mother.

Living in Dubai gave me the chance to showcase my hospitable nature and even stretched it a little. I concur with Ralph Waldo Emerson who said, 'The ornament of a house is the friends who frequent it'. Words so true.

Many of our friends came to visit us in Dubai. This was Dubai, who would not want to come? My house was always teeming with my inner circle of friends and still many of them were unable to visit before it was time to leave. Let us take a quick roll call.

The Folamis of Canada

We met the Folamis in Nairobi in 2001. Our families met for Christmas in Dubai and thoroughly enjoyed our time together. It was also a great time for our children to bond together again under one roof. We toured the Burj Khalifa and desert safari, we cruised the boat for dinners and enjoyed the man-made beaches together. Mrs. Folami visited the *gold souk* every morning in search of good bargains to make some money while holidaying in Dubai.

The Ogunleyes

These have been regular visitors wherever we moved to since our meeting in Belgium. They visited us in Romania, Switzerland, Dubai, and even Poland.

Sir Kay, as he is fondly called, likes to enjoy life and

luxury. He knows how to make money and how to enjoy it. His wife, my good friend, and I are birds of a kind; we flock together and share common views on things. This has intensified our friendship although sometimes, the sameness causes friction. We love our families and are committed to their well-being.

Sir Kay took us for dinner at the famous Burj Al Arab where a bottle of wine was more expensive than my bride price. Haha! We had a wonderful time that night with fond memories.

The Idowus

They are my 'Pam Pam' that I would not trade for anything. I am blessed to have Titi and Kunle as my family. First, Titi came into our lives, then Kunle and their children. These two have given everything to our friendship; they are dependable people — one you can trust with your life. To have friends like them is not easy, which is why I consider them a true blessing from the Lord.

Titi came with her children to visit us in Dubai. Her sister Mrs. Banke Adedapo and her son Isaiah also visited from the United States of America. We did dinner cruises, went to the safari, visited the malls, and went gold souk shopping. It was fun having them around. Mrs. Adedapo or Mummy Asa-sa, as we fondly call her, is calm, smart and a beautiful soul. Her fashion sense? Trendy, to say the least. I love having her around.

The Onos

Uncle Kenny came with Jeanie, his wife. They are our friends from Belgium. Uncle Kenny and Jeanie knew how to throw good owambes in our days in Belgium. Uncle is Nigerian and Jeanie is British, their combination is just fantastic. Great people to know!

Both heard from another friend that we were in Dubai, and they decided to spend some time with us even though their visit was purely for a personal holiday.

Seeing good old friends always brings out the memories of those wonderful days together.

The Kutis

Our friends from England also came for a wedding party/personal holiday in Dubai and we met up for an Arabian dinner. Although it was good, it turned out to be a mistake because Mr. Kuti would have preferred our Nigerian dinner after tasting the meal.

Most importantly we laughed, ate and enjoyed each other's company.

Eyinju

My friend from college heard I was in Dubai and called to tell me she was coming for the usual *karakata,* which is a Yoruba word for buying and selling. I was more than happy to see her in her usual bubbly mood. She *came correct,* as they say.

We shared a lot of laughs and cheerful hugs, reminiscing on our good old college days. We gisted for as long as there was something to talk about, then we had a sumptuous lunch with my family. That was the first time S.O. was meeting Eyinju. He was impressed with her cheerful disposition, and they soon struck it off as brother and sister.

Yeye knows her way well in Dubai, so she showed me where to buy things for personal use. It was she who organized everything for my birthday in 2020 — a boat cruise party in Dubai. She invited my husband and me for a wonderful dinner, an all-expense-paid night of enjoyment in the heart of Lagos, to say welcome back home to us. My very good-natured Eyinju, the Yeye Arobake of Ibaland, I love you.

The Jenyos

Mr. Jenyo my old schoolmate and his wife also stopped by from England to say hello to us. We went to the best African restaurant in Dubai — Kiza Restaurant and Lounge on Sheikh Zayed Road. We enjoyed their good cuisine and had something light to wash down the meal with. Mrs. Jenyo is an amiable personality to know.

The Ombus

We kind of hooked up first with Uncle, then his family came at different times. Though they were visiting for their private holidays, out of their good heart, they decided to say hello to us. Thank you, Uncle Emmanuel and Auntie Viola. I love you and wish you and your family all the best in life.

We hosted all these friends between September when we moved to our house and May when we left for another assignment. For me, it was great; it brought joy to my heart and lightened my spirit.

To have people that visit says a lot about my husband. I could not have opened my doors to them if he had said no or felt disturbed. He was working hard during the day and on most evenings, he would still take our guests out to have fun.

The Bible says he who must have friends must be friendly. We thank God for the many people we met along the way, our great friends who out of their love for us visited us in the Arabian desert, and for His provisions that enabled us to accommodate our teeming friends.

***

Some adventures do not last long. We had to move again. This time, to my favourite part of the world where I feel at home.

Dubai opened my eyes to a lot of things, one of which is that *not all that glitters is gold*. Dubai is not cheap to live in. Not anymore. Forget the tax-free slogan, you will pay for all the beautiful surroundings like you would do in any developed city.

In Dubai, decision making could be overwhelming. One is confronted with many choices. For example, to buy a car you will find numerous choices to pick from, and houses to rent are in different shapes and sizes. While freedom of choice is important to our wellbeing, too many choices can also lead to debilitating indecision.

I tucked two more lessons into my bag.

Firstly, a leader does not necessarily have to be far from his people to command respect. The United Arab Emirates leadership is down to earth with its people; it is democratic, transparent and welcoming in its general approach. 'The ruler should not have any barrier which separates him from his people.' This is a popular quote by Sheikh Zayed.

Secondly, a country can develop within the twinkle of an eye with visionary leaders to pilot its course. We see this first-hand in Dubai: a city that was transformed from the desert path of the past to the superhighway of the future.

POSTCARD FROM THE EXPAT'S WIFE

Upon arrival in the host location, get yourself a goal.

Sometimes, your spouse may not be supportive because they may not understand your struggles. You need to have a goal, especially if your spouse is not there for you. This will help you navigate the murky waters of being alone in a foreign land and help eliminate spousal resentment and relationship breakdown.

You need to ask yourself what you aim to achieve from the expatriate experience. In my case, it was good education and a balanced life for my children. I knew my husband could deliver at his job, and I did my best to help him focus. Thus, I became present in the children's schooling and activities; I volunteered in their schools, attended PTA events and befriended most of their teachers such that we were on a first name basis. Their friends became mine too.

Chapter Eight

MAYBE HOME

Wherever you go becomes a part of you somehow
~ Anita Desai

'Do you want to go to Poland? Why not choose another country?'

Once again, I was told many stories about Poland before we moved. One of my former schoolmates told me he had been to Poland and would not advise me to go there, but as we had always done, we simply followed the Lord's leading.

According to Wikipedia, a country that extends across the North European Plain from the Sudetes and Carpathian Mountains in the south to the sandy beaches of the Baltic Sea in the north.[6] The country is bordered by Lithuania and Russia to the northeast, Belarus and Ukraine to the east,

[6]https://en.wikipedia.org/wiki/Geography_of_Poland

Slovakia and the Czech Republic to the south and Germany to the west.

When we got to Poland, we discovered that it had changed so much since the country joined the EU. It is believed that when a country joins the EU, the union provides the country with funds to develop its infrastructure.

The same happened to Poland such that by the time we moved there, the country was undergoing a huge transformation and was no longer the former place people knew. The Poland we met was an exceptionally clean and well-maintained country with very kind and helpful people. It was also a cheap place to live in, and for me, that was the best deal. We settled in Warsaw.

Nobody should dismiss Poland from their list of European destinations to visit as it has much to offer curious and adventurous travellers.

Despite the widespread destruction of World War II, the country had several beautiful cities laid out with charming squares. Some cities had old towns with cobbled streets, Gothic churches and intriguing architecture alongside modern restaurants and a buzzing nightlife. The capital city of Warsaw and the nation's largest has grown into a huge metropolis with a cosmopolitan atmosphere.

Krakow, the second largest city, has an old town with cobbled streets and a grand castle. Wrocław is another delightful Polish city on the Oder River with bridges and lush parks along its banks.

Poland has a fascinating history and culture that shines brightly. There are many things that the nation takes pride in and here are just a few of them.

The Popular Wieliczka Salt Mine

The salt mine is one of Poland's most popular tourist attractions. Located just outside the city of Krakow, the mine is a UNESCO World Heritage site. It was an active mine from the Middle Ages up until 2007.

The mine has nine levels of galleries and is about 190 miles long. Around a million visitors explore it each year to admire the statues made of salt, the briny lake and rock salt chandeliers in the Chapel of Cunegonde. My family and I visited more than once. We had a first-hand experience and we loved taking our guests to enjoy the sight. Breathtaking indeed!

Kunle Idowu, Uncle Tunji Farinloye and others had the pleasure of visiting the salt mine with us; we had fun descending into the mine. Some of us took for granted the rigours involved in descending multiple steps to get into the salt mine. It was an adventure indeed.

Pope John Paul II

The man the world knows as Pope John Paul II is Karol Wojtyla, Poland's most famous citizen. He was the first non-Italian pope to serve since 1523 after Pope Adrian VI. Pope John Paul II worked diligently to end communism in Poland as well as across all of Europe. He is history's second longest-serving pope and was canonized as a saint in 2014. He served between 1978 and 2005.

There is a big statue of him near his ancestral home in Krakow. Our friends, Mr. & Mrs. Folami, visited us in Poland and had fun seeing the statue and having a tour of his family house. Mrs. Folami got a rosary for her mother from those teeming vendors outside the home.

Auschwitz Birkenau Museum

The Auschwitz Birkenau Museum is a silent monument to remind the world that the holocaust and World War II were one of history's darkest periods. A visit to the place tells a sad story, yet it is a well-respected and widely attended point of interest.

Visitors say it is an emotionally moving experience they would never forget. I remember breaking down in the middle of our tour crying my heart out. At a point, I took a break as I was gasping for breath at the sight of the horrific condition humans were subjected to. This kind of history must never be allowed to happen again. We all have a common duty to make every effort to avoid war. There are tons of evidence of the terrible human suffering caused by man's inhumanity to man in this museum.

During the holocaust, the site was turned into a concentration camp for Polish political prisoners by the Nazi occupation forces in 1939, which quickly garnered a reputation for brutality and sadism. Millions of people, mostly Jews, were taken there and imprisoned. The museum contains the original wooden barracks, gas chambers and memorabilia. It was a sober and a sad place to visit; one needs a large dose of courage to be able to visit the museum, not to talk of touring it.

I could not complete the tour, I felt sick to my

stomach and cried profusely. I did not go back there even when we had guests who wanted to visit. I always stayed back in the hotel in town.

Ceramics

Poland produces high quality dishwasher-safe ceramics and tableware. These pieces are painted with intricate patterns and are like pieces of fine artwork. They are available in large matching sets or individual pieces.

The smaller pieces are perfect as souvenirs, in case you visit Poland. The most popular brands are made in the Polish city of Boleslawiec. One downside to these works of art is that they are, of course, breakables.

I indulged myself and bought many sets of designs for my personal use. Make sure to ask to be served in one of my collections whenever you visit me in my country home.

Linens

Poland is well known as the producer of some of the world's finest linen products for tablecloths, runners, placemats, and napkins. These are made from strong and durable linens and come in beautiful patterns.

Linens are easy to pack and take home, so they make great souvenirs as well. They adorn my house in different colours. I love the materials and the fact that the designs are mostly handmade.

Pierogi

Pierogi or Polish dumplings are made of unleavened dough rolled extra thin and filled with a variety of fillings. The dumplings may be filled with meat, mushrooms and sauerkraut, sweetened cottage cheese or seasonal fruit. If filled with boiled potatoes and fried onions, they are known as Russian dumplings.

Pierogi is often served at Polish Christmas events as an appetizer, main dish or dessert depending on the fillings. They are either cooked in boiling water or pan-fried. I loved the pan-fried pierogi and enjoyed them better as a main dish rather than as a dessert.

Polish Vodka

It is an age-old debate between Russia and Poland on who has the best vodka, just as it is between Nigeria and Ghana on who makes the best jollof rice. Some say vodka was invented in Poland, so they have had a long time to perfect it. They base this view on the fact that the word 'vodka' appears in Polish Middle Age texts before the Cyrillic texts did in Russia. Others claim it is the kaleidoscope of flavours Polish vodka comes in that makes it better.

Many Poles love their vodka, especially in the winter months when the temperature decreases and the weather is ice cold. They take comfort in their vodka to keep warm.

***

Poland was a place we wanted to call home. We toyed with the idea of buying a home and settling down there as it is an affordable country. Buying a home there would have been an easy accomplishment, but my husband had become homesick and desired to return home after retirement. This was his long-term desire. We visited Nigeria quite often throughout our years of sojourn, but even more often when it was getting closer for us to draw the curtains.

Compared to the other European countries, I struggled with Polish language more than I did in the past with other countries I lived in. Polish had many words made up of consonants with no vowels. It was a difficult exercise and no matter how much I tried, I could not, so I gave up.

Nevertheless, it was in Poland I met some of the kindest people on earth. The people in Poland showed us love and hospitality. They are nice and helpful people. We went out and did a lot of fun activities together. I learned how to swim properly in Poland. I thoroughly enjoyed our stay in Poland, which was why I thought we should retire and stay there.

We did more than just touring and eating in Poland. I took over the church children's ministry and coordinated the department for more than two years. I also led a women's prayer group that met once a week for prayer and Bible study. I met weekly with other Christian ladies at another neighbourhood Bible study fellowship.

We had a good relationship with The Redeemed Christian Church of God (RCCG) in Warsaw as friends of the church and became friends with Pastor Zion and Mama Zion, the resident pastor and his dear wife. They are fantastic human beings and true children of God.

We also met others like Josh Anjorin and his family; Omoba the only African store CEO became a friend too with his lovely wife. My friend Marjana was my go-to whenever I needed any practical information. Marjana and I met in Bucharest and we met again in Poland, living again on the same street as we had done in Bucharest. The world is indeed a small place.

The coronavirus pandemic met us in Poland. It was a grey and depressing time. Everyone was locked in with no single soul on the street. At one point, the stadium was turned into a hospital.

I was confined to the four walls of my house, and it was not in my nature to be confined to a place. After two months, I became hysterical and started complaining to my husband.

'Are you not bored of staying indoors every day?' I asked one evening.

'Why?' he asked.

'I'm tired of staying indoors. I think we should go out. I am getting choked staying indoors.'

'But you know the rules. We are not allowed to go

out. COVID-19 is out there, and we can't risk it.' He tried to reason with me, but I would not have it.

'We will stay in our car and just drive around,' I nagged.

Due to my incessant pestering, he finally agreed, 'You won't give up. It's okay, we can take the risk.'

We heated the car which had been parked away all this while and drove out. 'Oh my God!' I cried when we saw the state of the outside world. It was deserted. I had never seen the city so empty like that before. It was a ghost town and that affected me badly.

During this time, we had to take turns getting groceries. Older people went in the morning and because I had grey hair, I kept my wigs away and went with the older people. The younger people had the afternoons to do their shopping.

Some of my friends that lived alone were deeply affected by the pandemic. I finally confirmed that God made us for interactions. We are social beings, hence we could not live in isolation, no matter what. It was hard for people to cope, a lot of them were getting depressed.

One of my neighbours, an Indian woman, called me one day, 'Kemi,' her sombre voice echoed over the phone. 'I'm coming to your house. I'm tired of being indoors,' she said in her Indian accent.

I was also desperate to talk to someone, but my husband would not permit anyone to come to our house. Not even the cleaner. He could not take the risk because older people were at higher risk of getting infected.

Over the phone, I said to my neighbour, 'I'm sorry but because of the covid restrictions we cannot receive visitors at the moment.'

She waited a few seconds before continuing, 'I will stay in front of your gate and we will talk to each other from there.' That was how desperate she was for someone's company. I could not stop her.

'Alright, I'll be waiting for you,' I replied. 'I also want to talk with someone apart from my husband.'

She came a few minutes later and we talked to each other from afar for about fifteen minutes until I got tired of the awkwardness of it all.

'You know what,' I said as I opened the gate, 'Just come in and let's talk while sitting.'

She came in and we went to my garden in the open air. We hugged each other and talked about anything and everything.

'I want to pray with you,' I said, seeking her permission. Even though she was Hindu, she agreed. So, we prayed.

COVID-19 killed many people. My souvenir from that period was an accumulation of fat that I still cannot lose because I ate without exercise. It was a very difficult period, which is why I am saddened by the Ukraine and Russia crisis. People are just getting over the shock of Covid-19 and barely recovering from its aftermath only to suddenly be faced with war.

Our stay in Poland came to an end in 2021 after an adventurous and memorable four years. I went back to Nigeria with my husband and a large box of treasured memories and lessons from my life as a traveller.

Some of the unforgettable lessons from Poland are that humans are the same, never to make assumptions, try something out, do something new and trust humanity. You must be open-minded, never say never and learn to experience the world with an interest to discover its goodness.

If you ever want to travel, just know that things cannot be the same where you are going as it is in your country. However, if you persevere and are patient enough, you will find out that the world is the same everywhere. It may take you a while to adjust but it will pay off in due course.

Finally, do not be like my friend who lived in the UK for ten years without ever trying pizza or a sandwich. Do not be so closed off from the world, acquire new knowledge, improve yourself and gain more wisdom. Whatever you cannot possibly change, learn to live with it.

POSTCARD FROM THE EXPAT'S WIFE

Upon arrival in your host location, socialize and network.

Communication is vital. Reach out to people and make new friends. Connect with and talk to others. You are not alone, there are many other people in your shoes. Join a group but be careful it is the right group for you. Make sure you are not bottling things up, share your thoughts and seek advice from professionals.

Chapter Nine

HOMECOMING

Why do you go away? So that you can come back. So that you can see the place you came from with new eyes and extra colours. And the people see you differently too. Coming back to where you started is not the same as never leaving.

~Terry Pratchett

My family is what you can call *Naija* birds; we are patriotic Nigerians. We love the country of our birth, we enjoy spending time there, and we love hanging out with our old friends and colleagues. Family is everything for us, so we never stayed away for too long at a stretch. We were either visiting for personal holidays or visiting for official business. Sometimes, people would see us and even assume that we never left, and this is also true for my children.

The love is unexplainable; my son abandoned his life in Canada to continue his career in Nigeria. My daughter returned for some internship with

Golden Effects Services Limited. You would always find me around my friends in and around Lagos. Therefore, it was a very easy decision for my husband to say Nigeria is home after retirement.

With so much going on in the country now, the insecurity, the economic crisis, and the unhealthy love of money by the younger generation, I can say that a lot has broken down culturally.

Culture shock. That might be the best way to describe how it feels to learn all over again to blend into a society I once knew. It has been tough but I am adjusting to all of it.

Back in Europe and in all the places we lived, shopping was a breeze. You only needed to go inside the supermarket, pick what you wanted and pay at the cashier. Here in Nigeria, you have to haggle to buy basic things. When we recently returned, I did not know how to buy anything anymore as butchers and meat sellers would try to cheat me. The open-air market is dreadful — pushing my way through throngs of people, haggling prices and being vigilant of being robbed at the same time. These were just too much for me to handle initially.

I also find driving more difficult because the roads are either bad or I have commercial bikers aka *okada* riders to contend with, and majority of them do not respect the traffic rules in Nigeria. Sometimes, I would wait to observe traffic lights while other drivers honk nonstop behind me. I would say under my breath 'You can honk all you want but I am not going anywhere until this light turns green.'

What about hiring artisans? One even made off with my money. I paid him a lot of money to work on something for me and that was the last time I ever saw him. When I confronted the person who brought him, he asked, 'Didn't you know him?'

I was livid. 'What do you mean by that? Were you not the person who recommended him?' I said.

He stood there, looking at me without shame or remorse until I told him to get out of my sight. This was too incredible for me to believe. I blamed myself for not asking him to sign a guarantor's form because I never thought I would be duped.

It has been tough adjusting to the realities here, where people bend the truth or outrightly prefer not to speak the truth. One time, I found a scratch on my car and I asked my driver, 'Na you hit person abi na dem hit you?'[7] All he could muster was a weak 'No' as if that was an explanation for the scratch on the car.

I find appalling the sense of entitlement some people have; they come asking with boldness as if they gave one any money to keep for them. Some of them would even borrow and refuse to pay back. Without shame, they would even return to borrow more and if one asked about the previous loan, one would become the enemy.

Then there is this thing of attending an *owambe* almost every week; I am getting tired of the narrative. Today it could be, 'Aunty Kemi, my cousin is burying his grandfather and we have picked *asoebi*.'[8] The next day it would be, 'My friend, my friend. My elder brother is getting married and we have picked *asoebi* for friends of the brother's sister.' By the time one calculates all the money spent on *asoebi*, one could start thinking of building one's first mansion because these *asoebi* are not cheap.

Imagine someone bringing a fifty-thousand-naira (₦50,000) fabric for me to buy without prior notice. The wastage and the inability of most

[7] Are you the one who hit the other car, or was it the other driver who hit yours?

[8] Asoebi is a uniform fabric worn by party attendees, common in the Yoruba tribe from which the word originates.

people to set their priorities right is just very disappointing.

I know that these parties enliven the soul but moderation in all things is key. In Europe, our white friends and colleagues would build a new house and move in without any pageantry; they would bury their parents and only serve sandwiches and tea, or even adopt a 'go get your own food' style.

Talking about outings, I cannot go out and stay late because of the insecurity issues in this country. Back in our international locations, I could drive at any time without fear.

What about attitude to time? People would give you an appointment for a certain time but three hours later, they have not shown up. 'I am coming' is an abused sentence here. When they tell you they are coming, just know they have not left their location.

Shall we talk about the matter of personal space? People disregard others' personal space without any thought to it. One time, we went out to eat and somebody poked her hand into my food.

'Wait a minute! Why did you do that?' I asked.

'What happened? Is it not my hand I put in your food? Do you think I have COVID?' She asked, indifferent.

'It's not right to do that, please. At least, you should have asked me or better still, used a fork.' I replied.

My correction fell on deaf ears. Her justification was that it would not be a big issue for her if I chose to poke my fingers into her food, after all, 'we are friends.'

Then there is the unchanging power cuts even after the name *NEPA* (National Electric Power Authority) has been changed numerous times. I brought my freezer from overseas and I hate what that appliance has had to go through due to the epileptic power supply. It is annoying that when the power is out, I would turn on the generator only to have the power restored immediately. The continuous back-and-forth wears me out and sometimes damages my appliances.

I call these experiences the *Naija* experience. Notwithstanding, I would not say that I have regrets because we made a conscious decision to come back home. Some of them are not strange to us as we had seen a lot from our visits in the past, they are only challenges and home is home. There's the hope that Nigeria will one day overcome these challenges when we know how to choose the right leaders, and when every citizen accepts that we are part of the problems and becomes ready for reorientation.

Despite all these challenges, I am happier in Nigeria than overseas with all the good life and luxuries. Nigeria has a way of making you happy irrespective of the challenges. I do not understand it myself, but I am happy dressing up, fixing my hair and putting on my makeup, especially the unbelievable makeovers.

Speaking of makeovers and makeup artists (MUA), I did a photoshoot for my birthday a while back and I could barely recognise myself after this young girl gave me a face beat. I could only mutter in awe, 'Is this me?'

I had a delightful photograph session and went home in high spirits. These sorts of things make one happy, and happiness elongates one's life.

If there is anything I have learned about my home country, it is that Nigeria has a way of balancing the stress it gives. Sometimes, I think it is the weather. Maybe the sunshine and the warmth cover for all its flaws and sends happiness coursing through my veins. Whatever the reason, I know that I was happy in Europe, but I am happier here and that is the bottom line.

POSTCARD FROM THE EXPAT'S WIFE

Upon arrival in the host location, protect your mental health. Should you experience feelings of anxiety or depression, seek help immediately. Irrespective of any stigma, your health is paramount.

Go out, make appointments to see professionals, consult therapists or talk to a good friend. Above all, pray ceaselessly. Tell it to God. Make Him your trusted friend.

Chapter Ten

LESSONS AND EVERLASTING MEMORIES

I am not the same, having seen the moon shine on the other side of the world.

~ Mary Anne Radmacher

Looking back on our journey these past two decades, I am compelled to take stock of some things that are worth sharing.

I found my entire experience beyond the shores of Nigeria interesting. In all these experiences, the most dramatic was Uzbekistan and that is because we became local superstars.

My most enjoyable place was Romania. I had so much fun swimming, going on outings and so much more. I lived in a compound of expatriates, where we did a lot of things together. There was a party every weekend and we chatted and laughed about our different cultures. Some of our neighbours who had been to Nigeria would narrate their horrible experiences to make fun of me and I would poke some at them too.

I have been in Amsterdam, Rome, London, New York and Toronto. These cities have their peculiarities and there are slums in every major city in the world.

The most challenging location was Belgium because it took me a while to find my foot there, but I finally did. As I said, you will always find stability at the end of the day.

I love Europe as I have come to understand the Europeans, their cultural values, intellectual curiosity, respect for others and tolerant nature. Even though it is one of the smallest continents in the world, it gave birth to what is now known as the Western civilization. Though I am not European, I see myself as one of them. Their simple lifestyle, living well without unnecessary attention and the availability of conditions essential for proper living standards; all of these appealed to me.

Leaving Nigeria exposed my family and me to the feeling of vulnerability repeatedly. The challenges of life on the road were numerous but the charm to this feeling was the joy of the adventures. We never felt sorry for ourselves, rather we felt and still feel privileged, blessed and empowered.

We learned so many languages that I almost forgot my native language. Most of the time, I mix the words up, confusing Russian for French in my head. I struggled a lot, particularly with the Polish language. It was nothing like I had ever studied or even heard, and I was constantly bamboozled. On many occasions, I bit my tongue or choked up trying frantically to pronounce a word. The combination of consonants without a vowel was a disaster for my head and mouth.

With too many languages clamouring for attention in my head, I decided to do my best in grasping just the essentials. I tried to at least learn to say good morning, hello and thank you. I was able to introduce myself and ask for reasonable assistance but other than that, I cherished my sanity.

My husband, on the other hand, did not bother with the languages; he concentrated on his powerful knowledge of the English language and would insist as if it was a right that an interpreter be provided for anyone who did not speak English. It worked for him most of the time.

My husband! He worked very hard, covering many different countries. Constantly busy and away from home, he became a symbol of what P&G stands for: excellence. If you gave my husband a job, you could as well go to sleep. If you entrusted something to him, it was as good as taken to the bank. The roles were challenging but through God's grace, he was able to do his best and I dare say that his best was the best known.

S.O. made sure we were all taken good care of. Wherever we went, his family came first. He never decided on our behalf but would always consult with us. It was open communication, love and respect that helped our children be who they are today.

Our son is now a powerful young man with a strong purpose in life. I have seen him achieve his goals, be vulnerable and still take strong decisions. I have nothing but love and respect for that.

Our daughter — beautiful and talented, very articulate, and has a good sense of understanding.

She has given us nothing but joy.

They are still a work in progress but in all, I am grateful to God for his grace, mercy and faithfulness.

Everything I experienced overseas shaped me, especially the concept of racism. When I arrived there, I only saw myself as a human and not as a Black woman but by the time I was leaving, something in me had changed. Honestly, if you are not strong-willed, when you encounter racism, it could kill everything in you as a person. If you do not control the self-pity that comes with being discriminated against, it could turn you into a weak and miserable person. I fell victim to this until I snapped out of it.

I discovered that every human being is vulnerable — black, white, brown, men, women, children, Christian, Muslims — everyone is vulnerable.

There are many rich and great cultures out there. Some cultures are similar to ours, while some are very different. Every human being holds their culture in high esteem and no culture is less than the other.

If there is any profound lesson I have learned on this journey, it is that regardless of the many things that make us different from one another, we are alike in a lot more ways. If you look deep enough, you will see the similarities in every human being, great or small, buttressing the biblical truth that we all came from the same Creator.

We are all human and have the same basic needs. Love is our paramount need and without it, nothing works. I have met many good-hearted people from every race.

Another true lesson I took from my sojourns was that evil has no gender or colour. It is not skin colour that makes one evil because I met good-hearted from every race, and I now live above prejudiced generalization. I also learned that humanity is far above wealth, and you must value relationship.

Imbibing the western culture also helped me to enjoy my space. In my culture, it is normal for someone to knock on your door at 2200 hours unannounced, but that never happened to us throughout our stay abroad because every visit was preceded with a notice.

I have also learned that in sharp contrast to the western world, some of our people abhor volunteering. After returning home, I registered as a volunteer with the Lagos Food Bank, a non-governmental organization (NGO) in Lagos. For many people, everything must come with payment, but there is joy in giving.

Ultimately, I can only say that it has been God on the heels of our journey. A chance opportunity that we thought would last only three years expanded to over two decades across seven countries.

He moved us from 32 degrees Celsius (32°C) in Nigeria to minus 28 degrees (-28°C) in Uzbekistan. On those cold days, my little daughter, all covered in sweaters and jackets would say, 'Mum, I'm walking like a penguin!' Beautiful memories.

We had our plans but God orchestrated his masterplan, and we did not have any choice but to let Him lead us as our Good Shepherd. We have a lot to be grateful for. For one, we were never admitted into any hospital for twenty-three years; we only visited for flus or some other minor illness that needed only medications. Most of the hospital budget was spent by me alone because I loved to go for routine checks. If I had a little headache, I always wanted to find out why.

In all our sojourn, faith and trust in God with buckets of prayer kept us through difficult times, sheltered us in moments of dire need and pointed us to the highway of decades-long enjoyment. We have enjoyed love, compassion, care, friendship and support from familiar faces and strangers alike.

Travelling is the soul of mastering the world and if given another chance, I will take this path again.

POSTCARD FROM THE EXPAT'S WIFE

- *Family is important and to keep it together, sacrifice is required.*
- *Change sometimes comes in the most unexpected ways. Be ready always and keep an open mind.*
- *With every change comes the need for adjustment. Adjustment is key for survival.*
- *Never make assumptions. There are good people everywhere.*

Goodbye to my Sunshine pre-school family.

In the classroom

Sunshine pre-school colleagues in Uzbekistan, 1999

MERICAN INTERNATIONAL

Certificate of Appreciation

This certificate is awarded to

Kemi Oloidi

On behalf of the Board of Directors and Students of AISB, thank you your valuable participation this year in Educational Po Committee. Your work has significantly strengthened our institution.

Keith Kirkham, EPC Chairperson — 5/23/2011

David Ottaviano, Director — 5/23/2011

AISB Education Policy Committee, 2011

Nigerian National Day in Bucharest 2010 (L-R Naty Tully, Ida Edwards, me, S.O. and Panos)

Lifesprings
International
Certificate of Completion
presented to
Kemi Oloidi
for the successful completion of all course work at the
Lifesprings School of Ministry Geneva
23 April, 2016 • Geneva, Switzerland

2016 Diploma program in Geneva

Proudly carrying the Nigerian flag to show respect and honour for my country, 2008

Classroom kids. Belgium, 2002

Picnic with friends

Saying goodbye to my church ladies in Warsaw, Poland

Certificate of Appreciation

This certificate is awarded to

KEMI OLOIDI

On behalf of the Board of Directors and Students of AISB, thank you for your valuable participation this year in Educational Policy Committee. Your work has significantly strengthened our institution.

Keith Kirkham, EPC Chairperson — Date

David Ottaviano, Director — Date

Certificate of Appreciation
AISB (American International School of Bucharest) 2010

Volunteer Summer Camp-
Crossroads Church Ferney France. 2014

S.O, our friend Laura from The Philippines and me

Dinner at mine (Couples' Evening on Valentine's Day)

International Day at AISB Bucharest 2010 (African hair braiding corner)

My Dami coming home for his NYSC

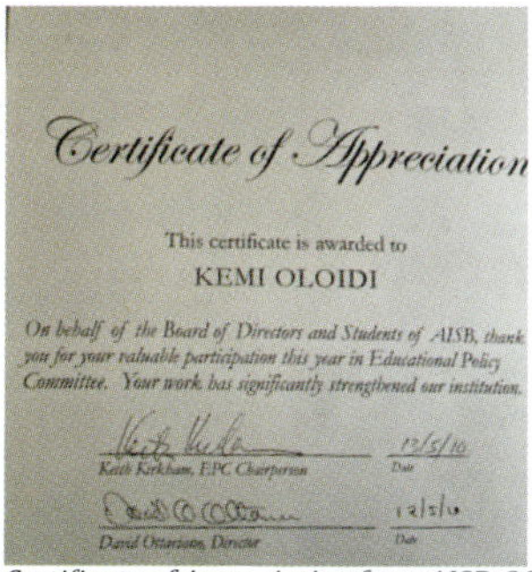

Certificate of Appreciation

This certificate is awarded to

KEMI OLOIDI

On behalf of the Board of Directors and Students of AISB, thank you for your valuable participation this year in Educational Policy Committee. Your work has significantly strengthened our institution.

Keith Kirkham, EPC Chairperson — 12/5/10 — Date

David Ottaviano, Director — 12/5/10 — Date

Certificate of Appreciation from AISB, 2010

My buddies in Bucharest

Watching a movie with Sunday school kids in International Christian Fellowship, Warsaw

Chapter Eleven

S.O.'S THOUGHTS

Many things have excited me in life: starting primary school, going into high school, having a first girlfriend, university life, getting my first job, my first flight and first trip abroad, among others. But none came close to the exciting life my family and I have had over the past twenty-three years.

Growing up in Nigeria is not bread and butter at all. I could have ended up as a carpenter, bricklayer, or tailor and many (especially those who are familiar with my background) would have still seen that as a major accomplishment for me. Everything I have achieved (including the man I have become) was by God's grace. Yes, I worked hard but that would not have amounted to much without the love, mercy, and grace of God over my life. I owe Him so much for crowning the little efforts I made with resounding success.

I met my wife by chance, or as some would say, rather unexpectedly. But once I laid my eyes on her, I knew she would be the mother of my children, a notion that was further confirmed when I had the chance to engage her in a brief discussion. I pursued her with vigour and thank God, she agreed to marry me. As they say, the rest is history. Now, we are blessed with two wonderful children and my wife is an honorary grandma.

Starting a career in the mid-80s was not easy as the government had just introduced the first structural adjustment program in Nigeria. However, God came through for me and created a way out of the employment wilderness of that time. I had a short stint as a research assistant then moved on to the civil service before going into the private sector. I wanted to be in sales (as that was the only job that comes with a company car) but ended up in human resources.

I will not bore you with the details of how that came to be, but I quickly realised that this is the career path that God had chosen for me. To equip myself for a role in Human Resources, I went back to university for a post-graduate degree in

Industrial & Labour Relations.

I worked in the areas of Employment, Labour and Human Resources for thirty-two years before retiring. During active service, we lived and worked in eight countries. In each country, I was in a multi-country leadership role that required extensive travels all the time.

Looking back, I can say with confidence that I had a successful career through the help of God Almighty and the support of my very capable wife. The saying, 'Behind every successful man, there is a strong woman,' could not be truer in our case. Kemi stood strong for me on the home front. Without the assurance that my home was in good hands, I would not have had the peace of mind to do a good job at work.

Raising children abroad was not easy as the system was not designed to inculcate in them the kind of African morals and values we held dear. However, Kemi did a fantastic job with the kids, especially during their formative years when I was globetrotting on business trips.

When she asked me to be a contributor in her book, she wanted me to write about my career and how the journey through many countries has shaped me. I could do that. However, there is nothing I would love to write about those years of sojourning other than her excellent contributions and support. She abandoned her career to become a trailing spouse. She gave up everything to build a lovely home for our family, so I believe this is a perfect opportunity to appreciate her and let her know how much I value and appreciate her love and sacrifices. It takes God's love and contentment for a woman like her to become like the biblical Ruth. My wife is truly phenomenal.

Through thick and thin, she stood strong. Doing her duties as a mother and a wife, she was always there, praying, fasting, supporting, trailing, and keeping everyone going. She became a pro in many areas: helping our children with their studies, taking them to swim practise, softball, basketball, gymnastics and many more. She managed the home front so excellently that I had no fears leaving her alone with the kids. That, in no small measure, helped my career as I was able to focus on delivering excellence at work where my contributions were exceptionally rewarded with many firsts amongst my Nigerian work colleagues.

The little I can therefore do is to use this opportunity to say a big THANK YOU! Thank you very much for pouring your life into our children and for making that tough but worthwhile investment. Thank you for all you do around the house. You do a great job of keeping our family organized. Thank you for all the times you have supported me. It has meant so much.

Thank you for being wise with our finances and agreeing with my decision all the time. Thank you for being you, for putting our family first, and for looking so gorgeous while you do it. Thank you for your faith in God and the confidence that together we belong like daffodils and butterfly. 'I love you' is the least I can say.

I also must not forget to write one or two things about our children. They made all the assignments easy for us: no tantrums, no drama. They were taught the way of the Lord and they did not depart from it. They worked hard to be who and where they are. Thank you for trusting our parenting skills. Yes, it was not without a hitch, but we scaled through. Everyone around us dreaded the teenage blues, but you both handled yourselves very well.

Thank you for respecting your mum and me. We love you both!

Sincerely,

Gbenga Oloidi

POSTCARD FROM THE EXPAT'S WIFE

- *We were made for interactions. Do not close yourself off from the world.*
- *Friendships bloom even in the most unlikely places. Keep an open mind.*
- *Travelling lets you see through the history and culture of other people, to appreciate diversity and differences.*
- *If you are fortunate enough, you will find someone who brightens your day and inspires you, someone who will always give you an ear regardless of the time, space or situation. That is the joy of friendship.*

Chapter Twelve

DAMILOLA'S THOUGHTS

For the better part of the past twenty years, my family has traversed life with the 'expat' label stuck firmly to our identity. As I ponder on what that label truly means, I think of the obvious differences between my family and the cultures we lived within but more importantly, I remember our openness to ingest the better parts of those cultures in a display of tolerance and humility. I also remember the many culture shocks we encountered, which made the pains that come with teenage years more intense at specific moments. The ups and downs of our expat experience create a Netflix-worthy stream of memories and a profound appreciation for life.

Sometimes, when I meet people who knew me during my early teenage years, they are astonished by my physical transformation which, though drastic, pales in comparison to my mental transformation throughout my expat experience.

As a pupil who stood out outwardly, I began my time in the American School in Bucharest with a sense of naivety at how different the treatment we received from others often was, from earlier seasons of our lives. My previous school environment was a true melting pot and I loved it there. However, in Bucharest, what I received was an inexplicable coldness that clearly professed my otherness to myself. It wasn't hell but it was still banishment. The following years were filled with many concessions of my true self, to keep myself emotionally safe, but at a cost.

You see, this part of my life exposed me to one of the greatest discoveries of my adolescence; that mental strength, confidence and kindness are the pillars of being truly seen for the wonderful human being one is, even to one's own self. This truth, I believe, is learnt by all of us within the span of our lives. However, as I look back now, it was pivotal for my trajectory that it dawned on me outside my homeland.

We are all susceptible to periods of doubt and fear, but it is our God-given duty to overcome such fears and stand firmly as the people we always intended to be.

Despite the seriousness of the previous paragraphs, my expat experience overflowed with so many funny and light-hearted moments. I remember ordering a pizza with my name—Damilola Oloidi—and seeing 'Fami Richards' on the pizza box when it arrived. I also remember being at a church potluck and watching non-Nigerians pour *draw soup* into a plate with jollof rice and salad before sitting down to look at the slimy mess they were expected to eat. I even recall a security guard at a store in Uzbekistan mistaking me for an urchin and denying me, a five-year-old, entry into a store despite seeing my Black parents walk in moments before me. Though scary as a child, I always remember with laughter how comical this moment would have looked to a bystander.

All in all, it has truly been a wonderful experience that I look forward to sharing with my future wife and children. The road may not have been easy, but as a family, we overcame every challenge thrown our way. I would be remiss not to acknowledge God's providence throughout our journey, a thought that comforts me as I move forward into new chapters of my life.

Dami

POSTCARD FROM THE EXPAT'S WIFE

- *If you want to live a happy life, do not dwell on things you cannot control.*
- *Having somewhere to go is home,; having someone to love is family and having both is a blessing. Never forget your family values.*
- *The way to confront any bias isn't by being angry but by consciously telling your story to help outsiders understand who you are.*
- *Our minds are capable of loving beyond boundaries. We are not different, we just have varied shades and colours.*

Chapter Thirteen

LIZZIE'S THOUGHTS

This book has been a long time coming. I remember being in high school and recognizing just how unique our life had been and how different it was from most people's life experiences. It is not easy growing up as a third culture (well, seventh, if we truly want to keep count) kid.

There is a comfort that comes from knowing there's so much of the world to see and despite the differences we share, we will always find people who understand us, culturally. And if we were to truly break things down further, our borders are manmade but our connection to humanity can never be broken, no matter how much borders may try to divide.

That is what growing up in Europe really taught me; borders are fake, and travel can open so many horizons for understanding. Ultimately, I think that is what growing up in our household taught me. No matter how many times we moved, I could never forget my Nigerian roots. Even with all these different cultures we were exposed to every few years, we were still, first and foremost, a Nigerian family, and nothing and no border could take that away. Instead, each border added to it: accents, languages, anecdotes, and memories that could fill a book.

I could argue that it was also a test of our cultural roots. How many cultures could we consider part of the mixture that forms our identity, our home? Is it the culture we gravitate to the most? There isn't really one; it is a melting pot and that is what Europe was for us and still is. Without getting into the full history and impact of colonialism and migration, forced or otherwise, on the continent, Europe has become the poster child for third culture-ism. You do not have to live an expatriate lifestyle to experience it. It is unlike anywhere else when it comes to that, especially North America.

One's sense of identity is not wrapped up only in the country of one's birth or the country represented at home, it is more than that. It is the comfort in knowing that as you grow, evolve and move, you have a network of people who impacted that growth and evolution, maybe even inspired it, all over the world.

One thing I miss the most about being an expat is the travelling; the privilege to be exposed to so much of what God has created in people and places. I used to live for the stories Dad would tell us of the different destinations he travelled to. One week in Cairo, another in Karachi, a layover in Casablanca, meetings in Paris, Zurich, Ohio. And I remember thinking 'I'll go there too, one day.' I'm grateful that some of those destinations have been checked off my travel bucket list.

With Mom, it has always been about family. Her love for our family is a constant stable. You know that no matter what, she has her family's back, and that is shown all over this memoir. Life with her is never dull and she made core memories even more colourful. I will always hold our trips to Overijse Park and Piscine every summer so dear to me. The rushing feeling that lingered for hours of riding the *rapids*; my mom watching us from the pool café above, with a book to entertain herself as she waved to my brother and me living our best lives.

After all the fun, she would help us change and get

ready to leave, but not before a snack from the café, which was usually a *jaw breaker*. I can still taste them now — pure sugar, without a particular taste, and would make my tongue numb from the constant licking — or the Australian ice cream place with the big scoop and the tangiest flavour.

Shall I talk about church? Each church was welcomed into our home. If there was not an already existing bible study my mom could host, she would create one and invite everyone to join.

Another thing I could never forget was how our home was always open. In every country we lived in, I have distinct memories of guests and dinner parties. Oh, how I love a good *Oloidi dinner party!* Every conversation ended in a history and political lesson on Nigeria, without fail. It became a running joke between my brother and me how long until the political debate started, usually at dinner and continued long after.

Our doors were always open, except on Halloween; the doors were closed then because we did not play those games.

It has been a good life, but not without the struggles. It is not easy packing up and moving.

Although there were the perks, as I have listed above, it was not always easy. There were the obvious struggles of language barrier, not finding our local foods and necessities. Then the deeper struggles of often being the odd ones out in a lot of spaces, especially when it comes to identity and racism in a world where we were just on the cusp of truly understanding diversity and inclusion.

Despite these struggles, my mom tried to leave her mark everywhere we went and in some places, she became a living legend. Projects she started continued even after she left. This is an accomplishment most of us chase our whole lives and here she was, doing it in her own way, my entire life.

I am glad that you are finally putting this all into writing, Mom; it has been a long time coming.

Love,
Lizzie (your favourite daughter)

POSTCARD FROM THE EXPAT'S WIFE

- *Ultimately, there is one God, one world, one humanity. You only need to open your eyes and see through the eyes of others.*
- *Do not be afraid of starting again. You never know the goodness that awaits you in the next phase.*
- *Opportunities to serve are often ways to learn and become your best self.*
- *We must not base our judgement about a whole country or continent on one encounter with one uninformed person. Keep an open and objective mind.*